Phr

GERMAN

With menu decoder, survival guide and two-way dictionary

Thomas Cook Publishing

www.thomascookpublishing.com

Introduction.......................5

Greetings............................9

Eating out..........................13

Shopping...........................29

Getting around..................37

Accommodation................43

Survival guide.................49

Emergencies.....................59

Dictionary........................63

Quick reference...............95

How to use this guide

The ten chapters in this guide are colour-coded to help you find what you're looking for. These colours are used on the tabs of the pages and in the contents on the opposite page and above.

For quick reference, you'll find some basic expressions on the inside front cover and essential emergency phrases on the inside back cover. There is also a handy reference section for numbers, measurements and clothes sizes at the back of the guide.

Front cover photography © Herbert Spichtinge / Zefa / Corbis
Cover design/artwork by Sharon Edwards
Photos: Jay M (p34), Melanie Tönnies (p38), Alexander Wallnöfer (p43),
Frank Burgey (p44), Martina Zirzuke (p58) and Jonathan Ruchti (p63)

Produced by The Content Works Ltd
www.thecontentworks.com
Design concept: Mike Wade
Layout: Tika Stefano
Text: Nina Stampfl
Editing: Helen Earis & Amanda Castleman
Proofing: Wendy Janes
Project editor: Begoña Juarros
Management: Lisa Plumridge & Rik Mulder

Published by Thomas Cook Publishing
A division of Thomas Cook Tour Operations Limited
PO Box 227, Unit 18, Coningsby Road
Peterborough PE3 8SB, United Kingdom
Company Registration Nº 1450464 England
email: books@thomascook.com
www.thomascookpublishing.com
+ 44 (0)1733 416477

ISBN-13: 978-184157-671-8

First edition © 2007 Thomas Cook Publishing
Text © 2007 Thomas Cook Publishing

Project Editor: Kelly Pipes
Production/DTP: Steven Collins

Printed and bound in Italy by Printer Trento

All rights reserved. No part of this publication may be reproduced,
stored in a retrieval system or transmitted, in any form or by any means,
electronic, mechanical, recording or otherwise, in any part of the world,
without prior permission of the publisher. Requests for permission
should be made to the publisher at the above address.

Although every care has been taken in compiling this publication, and
the contents are believed to be correct at the time of printing, Thomas
Cook Tour Operations Limited cannot accept any responsibility for
errors or omission, however caused, or for changes in details given in
the guidebook, or for the consequences of any reliance on the information provided. Descriptions and assessments are based on the author's
views and experiences when writing and do not necessarily represent
those of Thomas Cook Tour Operations Limited.

Introduction

Austria and Switzerland are popular skiing and walking destinations, but more and more Brits are discovering Germany's holiday charms. In fact, the country has a lot to offer between the North Sea and Lake Constance: wide, flat plains and medieval ports, plus vineyards, castles and alpine lakes.

Wherever you wander, a few German phrases will ease the trip. Often underestimated, this language is the mother tongue of more than 100 million Europeans.

So drop the **angst**, leave the children in the **kindergarten**, pack your **rucksack** and then enjoy a **frankfurter** or a **pretzel** in the **biergarten**!

The basics

The language is part of the West Germanic sub-group and ultimately traces back to Indo-European. It shares roots with English, Dutch, Afrikaans, Yiddish and Frisian. Many words sound familiar to English-speakers, in fact:

word – **das Wort**	here – **hier**	garden – **der Garten**
hand – **die Hand**	milk – **die Milch**	glass – **das Glass**
house – **das Haus**	shoe – **der Schuh**	land – **das Land**

German has also borrowed some of our vocabulary. Terms such as 'computer', 'teenager' or 'marketing' are used in everyday speech. However, guard against 'false friends', words that appear similar or even identical in German, but have other meanings entirely:

sensible	**– sensible**	(sensitive)
wink	**– winken**	(to wave)
to become	**– bekommen**	(to get)
brave	**– brav**	(good, well-behaved)
chef	**– der Chef**	(boss)
gift	**– das Gift**	(poison)
art	**– die Art**	(kind, type)
handy	**– das Handy**	(mobile phone)

The world's longest words

German is notorious for its compound words. Nouns link together like train carriages into long, connecting strings, creating words like **Fußballweltmeisterschaftsqualificationsspiel** (footballworld championship qualification game). Take a deep breath!

The interrogatives 'who' and 'where' are tricky too; they become respectively **wer** and **wo**, which can be misleading.

German is the official language in Germany and Austria, and one of four national tongues in Switzerland. The varied and numerous dialects often challenge students. The strongest is probably **Schwyzerdütsch** (Swiss German), though Austrian and southern German varieties can be tough. But don't let this intimidate you. Just ask: **Können Sie bitte langsamer sprechen?** (Could you please speak more slowly?). Your conversation partner will most likely switch to 'proper' German – or try to, at least.

Grammar

The German language has three genders: masculine, feminine and neuter. The articles – **der, die, das** – reflect this:

der Vater (father)	**die Mutter** (mother)	**das Kind** (child)
der Löffel (spoon)	**die Gabel** (fork)	**das Messer** (knife)

Verb endings change to show who is doing the action – and when. Here's an example of the verb **gehen** (to go):

ich	**geh-e**	I go
du	**geh-st**	you go
er, sie, es	**geh-t**	he, she goes
wir	**geh-en**	we go
ihr	**geh-t**	you go
sie	**geh-en**	they go

From here, the rules grow more complex. But no need to worry about nominatives and accusatives, irregular and reflexive verbs, now. Memorise a few simple phrases to ease your travels and make foreign friends.

Pronunciation

Unlike its grammar, German pronunciation is quite straightforward. Mainly, say what you see. However, there are some **umlaut** vowels and vowel combinations not used by English:

ä as in	**verspätet** (delayed) or **Mädchen** (girl)	pronounce like **ai in** fair or **a** in day
ü as in	**kühl** (cool) or **Büro** (office)	Say a long **ee** and then round lips to a long **oo**
ö as in	**mögen** (to like) or **Frisör** (hairdresser)	pronounce like the **oe** in Goethe (similar to the **u** in turn)

äu or eu as in	**Räume** (rooms) or **heute** (today)	pronounce like **oy** in toy or joy
ei as in	**mein** (my) or **schneiden** (to cut)	pronounce like **i** in fine or mine
ß as in	**Straße** (street) or **groß** (big, tall)	pronounce like **ss** in boss or asset

Basic conversation

Hello	**Hallo/Guten Tag**	_halloh/gooten taag_
Goodbye	**Tschüss/Auf Wiedersehen**	_chewss/owf veederzane_
Yes	**Ja**	_yaah_
No	**Nein**	_nine_
Please	**Bitte**	_bittuh_
Thank you	**Danke**	_dankuh_
You're welcome	**Keine Ursache/ gerngeschehen**	_kynuh uhrsaachuh/ gern guhschayhen_
Sorry	**Entschuldigung/ Verzeihung**	_entschuldigung/ fertsighung_
Excuse me (apology)	**Entschuldigung**	_entschuldigung_
Excuse me (to get attention)	**Entschuldigen Sie**	_entschuldigen zee_
Excuse me (to get past)	**Verzeihen Sie**	_fertsighen zee_
Do you speak English?	**Sprechen Sie Englisch?**	_sprekhen zee ennglissh?_
I don't speak German	**Ich spreche nicht Deutsch**	_ish sprekhuh nikht doitsch_
I speak a little German	**Ich spreche ein wenig Deutsch**	_ish sprekhuh eyn vehnig doitsch_
What?	**Wie bitte?**	_vee bittuh?_
I understand	**Ich verstehe**	_ish ferschtayhuh_
I don't understand	**Ich verstehe nicht**	_ish ferschtayhuh nikht_
Do you understand?	**Verstehen Sie?**	_ferschtayhen zee?_
I don't know	**Ich weiss nicht**	_ish vice nikht_
I can't	**Ich kann nicht**	_ich kann nikht_
Can you please speak more slowly?	**Können Sie bitte langsamer sprechen?**	_kernen zee bittuh langsaamuh sprekhen?_
Can you please repeat that?	**Können Sie das bitte wiederholen?**	_kernen zee dass bittuh veederholen?_

Greetings

German is definitely not an easy
language, given its different
articles and the ever-changing
endings of verbs and nouns. Thus
any foreigner's effort to speak is
much appreciated. In most parts of
Germany, the 'proper' German is
spoken; called **Hochdeutsch** (High
German), it's the tongue taught
abroad – and also the straight
pronunciation used in this book.
The problems start in the south.
The strong dialects of Bavaria,
Austria and Switzerland at times
sound like other languages.
However, **Hochdeutsch** is
understood everywhere.

Meeting someone

Hello	**Hallo**	_halloh_
Hi	**Hallo**	_halloh_
Good morning	**Guten Morgen**	_gooten morgen_
Good afternoon	**Guten Tag**	_gooten taag_
Good evening	**Guten Abend**	_gooten ahbent_
Sir/Mr	**Herr**	_hair_
Madam/Mrs	**Frau**	_frau_
Miss	**Frau**	_frau_
How are you?	**Wie geht es Ihnen?**	_vie gayt es eenen?_
Fine, thank you	**Gut, danke**	_goot, dankuh_
And you?	**Und Ihnen?**	_unt eenen?_
Very well	**Sehr gut**	_zehr goot_
Not very well	**Nicht sehr gut**	_nikht zehr goot_

Hail and well met

In the south of Germany and in Austria, **Hallo** (hello) and **Guten Tag** (good day) are usually replaced by **Servus** or **Grüß Gott**. At the Swiss border, **Grüezi** becomes more common.

Small talk

My name is...	**Ich heiße...**	_ish highsuh..._
What's your name?	**Wie heißen Sie?**	_vee highssen zee?_
I'm pleased to meet you!	**Sehr erfreut!**	_zehr erfroyt!_
Where are you from?	**Woher kommen Sie?**	_vohair kommen zee?_
I am from Britain	**Ich komme aus Britannien**	_ish kommuh owss britaannyen_

Do you live here?	**Leben Sie hier?**	*lehben zee heeuh?*
This is a great country	**Das ist ein tolles Land**	*dass isst eyn tolluhs lant*
This is a great city/town	**Das ist eine tolle Stadt**	*dass isst eyenuh tolluh schtadt*
I am staying at...	**Ich wohne in...**	*ish vohnuh in...*
I'm just here for the day	**Ich bin nur für den Tag hier**	*ish bin nur fuer deyn taag heeuh*
I'm here for...	**Ich bin hier für...**	*ish bin heeuh fuer...*
- a weekend	**- ein Wochenende**	*- eyn vochenenduh*
- a week	**- eine Woche**	*- eyenuh vochuh*
How old are you?	**Wie alt sind Sie?**	*vee alt zint zee?*
I'm... years old	**Ich bin... Jahre alt**	*ish bin... yahruh alt*

Family

This is...	**Das ist...**	*dass isst...*
- my husband	**- mein Ehemann/Gatte**	*- mine ehhuhman/gattuh*
- my wife	**- meine Frau/Gattin**	*- mynuh frau/gattin*
- my partner	**- mein Partner**	*- mine partner*
- my boyfriend/ girlfriend	**- mein Freund/ meine Freundin**	*- mine froynt/ mynuh froyntin*
I have...	**Ich habe...**	*ish hahbuh...*
- a son	**- einen Sohn**	*- eyenen zohn*
- a daughter	**- eine Tochter**	*- eyenuh tokhter*
- a grandson	**- einen Enkelsohn**	*- eyenen enkelzohn*
- a granddaughter	**- eine Enkeltochter**	*- eyenuh enkeltokhter*
Do you have...	**Haben Sie...**	*hahben zee...*
- children?	**- Kinder?**	*- kinder?*
- grandchildren?	**- Enkelkinder?**	*- enkelkinder?*
I don't have children	**Ich habe keine Kinder**	*ish hahbuh kynuh kinder*
Are you married?	**Sind Sie verheiratet?**	*zind zee ferhighraatet?*
I'm...	**Ich bin...**	*ish bin...*
- single	**- ledig/single**	*- laydig/single*
- married	**- verheiratet**	*- ferhighraatet*

| - divorced | **- geschieden** | - guh_scheed_en |
| - widowed | **- verwitwet** | - fer_vit_vet |

Courtesy counts

Add a polite **bitte** (please) to any request, as is customary in German-speaking countries. If you're grateful, respond with **Danke schön**, **Danke sehr** or **Vielen Dank** – all variants on 'thanks so much'.

Saying goodbye

Goodbye	**Auf Wiedersehen**	owf _veed_erzane
Good night	**Gute Nacht**	_goot_e nakht
Sleep well	**Schlafen Sie gut**	_schlaaf_en zee goot
See you later!	**Bis später!**	biss _spay_tuh!
Have a good trip!	**Gute Reise!**	_goot_uh _righ_suh!
It was nice meeting you	**Es war nett Sie kennenzulernen**	ez var nett zee _kenn_entsuelernen
All the best!	**Alles Gute!**	_all_uhs _goot_uh!
Have fun!	**Viel Spaß!**	feel schpaass!
Good luck!	**Viel Glück!**	feel glueck!
Keep in touch	**Bleiben Sie in Kontakt**	_bly_ben zee in con-tact
My address is...	**Meine Adresse lautet...**	_my_nuh ad_dress_uh _lout_et...
What's your	**Wie lautet Ihre...**	vee _lout_et _ihr_uh...
- address?	**- Adresse?**	- ad_dress_uh?
- email?	**- E-mail-Adresse?**	- e-mail ad_dress_uh?
- telephone number?	**- Telefonnummer?**	- tele_fohn_nummuh?

Eating out

German cuisine has distinct regional flavours, but the common denominators are delicious sausages and filling roasts. Foreign influences have spiced menus, especially in border areas. Fine pasta dishes draw on Italian expertise, for example, and the favourite fast food, doner kebab, is of Turkish origin.

The Austro-Hungarian monarchy left its mark on Austrian cuisine. Dishes from neighbouring Hungary and Bohemia include sweet and savoury dumplings, goulash and curd cheese desserts. In Switzerland it's all about cheese: think fondues galore.

Introduction

Coffee bars, bistros and **Kneipen** (pubs) offer snacks to soothe a small appetite. Hot lunches in restaurants are usually served between 11.30am and 2.30pm. Watch out for good dish-of-the-day deals. In-vogue restaurants are likely to be fully booked in the evenings, especially towards the weekend.

I'd like...	**Ich hätte gerne...**	*ish hettuh gernuh...*
- a table for two	**- einen Tisch für zwei**	*- eyenen tisch fuer tsvigh*
- a sandwich	**- ein Sandwich**	*- eyn zandveesh*
- a coffee	**- einen Kaffee**	*- eyenen caffay*
- a tea (with milk)	**- einen Tee (mit Milch)**	*- eyenen tay (mit milkh)*
Do you have a menu in English?	**Haben Sie eine Speisekarte auf Englisch?**	*hahben zee eyenuh schpysuhkartuh owf ennglissh?*
The bill, please	**Die Rechnung bitte**	*dee reshnung bittuh*

You may hear...

Raucher oder Nichtraucher?	*rowkuh oduh nikhtrowkuh?*	Smoking or non-smoking?
Was hätten Sie gerne?	*vass hetten zee gernuh?*	What are you going to have?

Germanic cuisines

German specialities

Although Germany's regions have their own culinary traditions, many specialities are popular throughout the country. Dialects sometimes refer to the dishes by different names, though, and ingredients might change from one state to the other. The variation is all part of the fun.

Reibekuchen/ Kartoffelpuffer	*righbuhkoochen/ katoffelpuffuh*	Potato pancakes with apple sauce
Kohlroulade/ Krautwickel	*kohlroulaaduh/ krowtvickel*	Meat wrapped in cabbage leaves
Hasenpfeffer	*haasenpfeffuh*	Peppered hare stew
Sauerbraten	*zowuhbraaten*	Marinated, pot-roasted beef

North Germany

Fish and seafood dishes are most typical for this coastal region. Close to the island of Sylt, oysters are a delicacy. However, the north Germans also like meat and venison, come autumn. Expect warm, filling dishes: food to ward off the wind's chill.

The Germans' favourite fast food
Legend claims that Turkish immigrants invented the döner kebab in Berlin Kreuzberg back in the 1970s. Now it's Germany's favourite fast food dish, more popular even than burgers.

Signature dishes
(see the Menu decoder for more dishes)

Aalsuppe	_aaahlzuppuh_	Eel soup
Labskaus	_labscowse_	Corned beef with beet and potatoes
Pinkel	_pinkel_	Smoked pork and oat sausage

Rhineland

The citizens of Cologne and the Rhineland are a distinct people with comical names, not only for their dishes. To order a beer, ask the **Köbes** (waiter) for a **Kölsch**, the famous beer brewed in Cologne.

Signature dishes
(see the Menu decoder for more dishes)

Suurbrode (Rheinischer Sauerbraten)	_zuhrbroduh (rhignishhuh zowuhbraaten)_	Roast marinated beef or horse meat
Himmel un Ääd (Himmel und Erde)	_himmel un ehd (himmel unt erduh)_	Fried black pudding with mash and apple puree
Kölsch Kaviar	_kerlsch kaviar_	Black pudding with rye bread

Thuringia

The Thuringians have a rich cuisine, known for its many sausage varieties and heavy meat dishes. Venison specialities are also typical for this area. The cakes are exemplary, especially **Schmandkuchen**, made with seasonal fruits.

Signature dishes
(see the Menu decoder for more dishes)

Schniedle und Schwammle	_schneedluh unt schvammluh_	Vegetable soup with mushrooms
Mutzbraten	_mutzbraaten_	Birch-roasted pork
Thüringer Rostbrätel	_tueringuh rostbraytel_	Marinated, barbecued pork

Bavaria

Bavarian cuisine has its roots in peasant cooking and thus tends towards the simple, hefty side of the spectrum. Try the typical sweet dishes, which can easily double as a solid meal. Bavaria is, of course, beer country and the locals are particularly fond of their 'pure' brews.

Signature dishes
(see the Menu decoder for more dishes)

Weißwurst mit Breze	_vicevurst mit brehtsuh_	White sausage, a pretzel, mustard
Pichelsteiner Eintopf	_pikhelschtynuh eyntopf_	Meat and vegetable stew
Dampfnudeln	_dampfnoodeln_	Sweet dumplings

Beer in the garden

Locals love to meet their friends after work in a cosy **Biergarten**. Most typical in Bavaria, they're also found elsewhere in the region, offering the best local food specialities.

Swabia

Swabian cuisine overspills into nearby Austria and Switzerland. **Spätzle** – tiny, pasta-like balls of dough – is the most characteristic local dish, served as a side, a main baked with cheese, or in soup. A good, homemade fruit **schnapps** helps to digest the heaviness.

Frankfurt's most famous dish
Frankfurter Grüne Sauce (green sauce) is a dish popular in the whole state of Hesse. Made of meat and fresh herbs, it's served with potatoes and hardboiled eggs.

Signature dishes

(see the Menu decoder for more dishes)

Flädlesuppe	*flehdelzuppuh*	Consommé with thin pancake strips
Kässpätzle	*kaysschpetzluh*	Pasta with cheese
Schupfnudeln	*schupfnoodeln*	Potato pasta

Austrian specialities

Austrian dishes are strongly influenced by Bohemian and Hungarian cuisines and – in some parts – also envelop Italian cooking traditions. Pudding fans will love **Mehlspeisen**: sweet, flour-based dishes unknown to the rest of the world.

Signature dishes

(see the Menu decoder for more dishes)

Wiener Schnitzel	*vienuh shnitsul*	Breaded veal
Tafelspitz mit Bratkartoffeln und Spinat	*tarfulshpits mit bratkartoffln unt shpinat*	Beef, fried potatoes, spinach and sauces
Backhendl	*bakhendl*	Breaded chicken
Kaiserschmarrn mit Zwetschkenröster	*kiyzershmarn mit tsvetshkenrushtuh*	Scrambled pancake, plum jam

Swiss specialities

Unsurprisingly, Switzerland's national dishes are predominantly cheese-based. Originally from the country's west, **Rösti** has also become popular countrywide.

Signature dishes
(see the Menu decoder for more dishes)

Zürcher Geschnetzeltes	_tsoorkhuh gshnetzeltes_	Chopped veal with a cream sauce
Raclette	_raklet_	Melted cheese, potatoes, pickles
Älplermagronen	_epluhmagrohnun_	Macaroni, onions, potatoes, cheese with creamy sauce

Hard cheese

Nowadays, every family and restaurant has its own **fondue** recipe. It's a far cry from the dish's origin, when hard bread was dipped into melted stale cheese to overcome tough alpine winters. A word of warning: lose what you're dipping and the next drinks are on you!

Wine, beer & spirits

Germany and Austria are – without doubt – beer countries, possibly _the_ beer countries. All regions brew some variety: wheat, dark or clear, all excellent. But don't forget the wines (more white than red), the delicious **schnapps** and the unique brandy, **Asbach Uralt**.

Pharisäer	_farisayuh_	Coffee, rum, cream
Appelkorn	_appelkorn_	Apple and wheat liqueur
Birnenschnapps	_birnenschnaps_	Pear schnapps

Best quality sweet wine
Trockenbeerenauslese is a sweet wine made from grapes that dried and sweetened on the vine. Only selected grapes make the cut. The high quality **Auslese** is usually served as a dessert wine.

Riesling	_reeceling_	Typical white wine
Could I have...	**Könnte ich... haben?**	_kerntuh ish... hahben?_
- a beer?	**- ein Bier?**	_- eyn beeuh?_
- a glass/a bottle of white/red/rosé wine?	**- ein Glas/eine Flasche Weiß-/Rot-/Roséwein**	_- eyn glahs/eyenuh flaschuh vice-/roht-/rosayvine_
- a glass/a bottle of champagne?	**- ein Glas/eine Flasche Champagne**	_- eyn glahs/eyenuh flaschuh champahgnyuh_

You may hear...

Was darf ich Ihnen servieren?	_vass darf ish eenen zerveeren?_	What can I get you?
Wie hätten Sie es gerne?	_vee hetten zee ez gernuh?_	How would you like it?
Mit oder ohne Eis?	_mit ohduh ohnuh ice?_	With or without ice?
Kalt oder in Zimmertemperatur?	_kalt ohduh in tsimmuhtemperaator?_	Cold or room temperature?

Snacks & refreshments

Snacks range from fresh **Fischbrötchen** (bread roll with fish) at a northern market to **Wurstsalat** (sausage salad) or **Bierradi** (thin-sliced radish) in a southern beer garden. Döner kebabs remain hugely popular, as do pretzels.

Kaffee und Kuchen	_caffay unt koochen_	Coffee and cake
Belegte Brötchen	_belehgtuh brertchen_	Open sandwiches

Strammer Max	*schtramm*uh max	Bread with ham and a fried egg
Gulaschsuppe	*goo*lasch*zupp*uh	Goulash soup
Wiener Würstchen mit Senf und Brot	*vee*nuh *vuer*schten mit zenf unt broth	Sausages with mustard and bread

Vegetarians & special requirements

I'm vegetarian	**Ich bin Vegetarier/in**	*ish bin vegetareeuh/in*
I don't eat...	**Ich esse...**	*ish essuh...*
- meat	**- kein Fleisch**	*- kyn flysch*
- fish	**- keinen Fisch**	*- kynen fisch*
Could you cook something without meat in it?	**Könnten Sie etwas ohne Fleisch zubereiten?**	*kernten zee etvass ohnuh flysch tsuberighten?*
What's in this?	**Was ist da drinnen?**	*vass isst dah drinnen?*
I'm allergic to...	**Ich bin allergisch gegen...**	*ish bin allergish gehgen...*
-nuts	-Nüsse	*- nuessuh*
-gluten	-Gluten	*- glooten*
-dairy	-Laktose	*- laktozuh*

Children

Are children welcome?	**Sind Kinder willkommen?**	*zint kinder villkommen?*
Do you have a children's menu?	**Haben Sie eine Kinderspeise- karte?**	*hahben zee eyenuh kinderschpysuh- kartuh?*
What dishes are good for children?	**Welche Gerichte sind für Kinder gut?**	*velchuh gerischtuh zint fuer kinder goot?*

Smoked eel and fresh crabs

The fish market is Hamburg's biggest shopping attraction on Sundays. Seafood lovers prowl among the heaped stalls. Rise early to join them: it closes at 10am.

Menu decoder

Essentials

Breakfast	**das Frühstück**	*dass fruehschtueck*
Lunch	**das Mittagessen**	*dass mittaagessen*
Dinner	**das Abendessen**	*dass ahbentessen*
Cover charge	**der Gedeckpreis**	*der guhdeckprice*
VAT inclusive	**Inklusive Mehrwertsteuer**	*inkloosivuh mehrvertstoyuh*
Service included	**Service inbegriffen**	*serveecesuh inbegriffen*
Credit cards (not) accepted	**Kreditkarten (nicht) akzeptiert**	*kraydeetkarten (nikht) aktsepteeert*
First course	**der erste Gang/ die Vorspeise**	*der erstuh gang/dee forschpysuh*
Second course	**der zweite Gang/ das Hauptgericht**	*der tsvightuh gang/dass howptguhrischt*
Dessert	**das Dessert/die Nachspeise**	*dass dessert/dee nakhschpysuh*
Dish of the day	**das Tagesgericht**	*dass taagguhsguhrischt*
House specials	**die Spezialitäten des Hauses**	*dee spetsiaalitaeten des howzuhs*
Set menu	**das (Tages-)Menü**	*dass (taagguhs-)menew*
À la carte menu	**das Menü à la carte**	*dass menew à la carte*
Tourist menu	**das Gästemenü**	*dass gestuhmenew*
Wine list	**die Weinkarte**	*dee vinekartuh*
Drinks menu	**die Getränkekarte**	*dee guhtrenkuhkartuh*
Snack menu	**die Imbisskarte**	*dee imbisskartuh*

Methods of preparation

Baked	**Gebacken**	*guhbacken*
Boiled	**Gekocht**	*guhkochkt*
Braised	**Geschmort**	*guhschmort*
Breaded	**Paniert**	*paneeert*
Deep-fried	**Frittiert**	*friteeert*
Fresh	**Frisch**	*frisch*
Fried	**Gebraten**	*guhbraaten*
Frozen	**Gefroren**	*guhfroren*
Grilled/broiled	**Gegrillt**	*guhgrillt*

Meat is not a must

Though meat plays a vital role in German cuisine, vegetarian restaurants are emerging, especially in the cities. Even traditional menus often include some **vegetarische Speisen**. Asian takeaways are good standbys too.

Marinated	**Mariniert**	*marineeert*
Mashed	**Püriert**	*puereeert*
Poached	**Pochiert**	*pocheeert*
Raw	**Roh**	*roh*
Roasted	**Geröstet**	*guhrerstet*
Salty	**Salzig**	*zaltsig*
Sautéed	**Sautiert**	*zorteeert*
Smoked	**Geräuchert**	*guhroyschert*
Spicy (flavour)	**Würzig**	*vuertsig*
Spicy (hot)	**Scharf**	*schaarf*
Steamed	**Gedämpft**	*guhdempft*
Stewed	**geschmort**	*guhschmort*
Stuffed	**Gefüllt**	*guhfuellt*
Sweet	**Süß**	*zuess*
Rare	**Blutig (gebraten)**	*blootig (guhbraaten)*
Medium	**Rosa gebraten**	*rohsa guhbraaten*
Well done	**Gut durchgebraten**	*goot dorchguhbraaten*

Common food items

Beef	**Das Rindfleisch**	*dass rintflysch*
Chicken	**Das Huhn**	*dass hoon*
Turkey	**Der Truthahn**	*der troothaahn*
Lamb	**Das Lammfleisch**	*dass lammflysch*
Pork	**Das Schweinefleisch**	*dass schvynuhflysch*
Fish	**Der Fisch**	*der fisch*
Seafood	**Die Meeresfrüchte**	*dee mehrruhsfrueschtuh*
Tuna	**Der Thunfisch**	*der toonfisch*
Beans	**Die Bohnen**	*dee bohnen*
Cheese	**Der Käse**	*der kaysuh*
Eggs	**Die Eier**	*dee eyeuh*
Lentils	**Die Linsen**	*dee linzen*
Pasta/noodles	**Die Pasta/ die Nudeln**	*dee pasta/ dee noodeln*
Rice	**Der Reis**	*der rice*
Cabbage	**Der Kohl**	*der kohl*
Carrots	**Die Karotten**	*dee karotten*
Cucumber	**Die Gurke**	*dee gorkuh*
Garlic	**Der Knoblauch**	*der knohblowch*
Mushrooms	**Die Pilze/die Champignons**	*dee piltsuh/dee champinyons*
Olives	**Die Oliven**	*dee oleeven*
Onion	**Die Zwiebel**	*dee tsveebel*
Potato	**Die Kartoffel**	*dee kartoffel*
Red/green pepper	**Die rote/grüne Paprika**	*dee rohtuh/gruenuh papreeka*
Tomato	**Die Tomate**	*dee tohmaatuh*
Vegetables	**Das Gemüse**	*dass gemuesuh*
Bread	**Das Brot**	*dass broht*
Oil	**Das Öl**	*dass erl*
Pepper	**Der Pfeffer**	*der pfeffuh*
Salt	**Das Salz**	*dass zalts*
Vinegar	**Der Essig**	*der essig*
Cake	**Der Kuchen**	*der koochen*
Cereal	**Die Getreideflocken**	*dee guhtryduhflocken*
Cream	**Die Sahne**	*dee zahnuh*

Fruit	**Das Obst**	*dass ohbst*
Ice cream	**Das Eis**	*dass ice*
Milk	**Die Milch**	*dee milkh*
Tart	**Die Torte**	*dee tortuh*

Most of the dishes below are German but will be found in parts of Austria and Switzerland; those found predominantly in Austria and Switzerland are marked with (A) or (CH) respectively.

First course dishes

Erbsencremesuppe	*erbsencremzuppuh*	Cream of pea soup
Kartoffelsuppe (mit Brotcroutons)	*kartoffelzuppuh (mit brohtcroutons)*	Potato soup (with croutons)
Hering mit roter Beete	*hehring mit rohtuh behtuh*	Herring with beetroot
Geräucherter Lachs mit Senf-sauce und Toast	*guhroyschuhtuh lakhs mit zenfzor-suh unt toast*	Smoked salmon with mustard sauce and toast
Salatteller	*zalaattelluh*	Salad plate
Leberknödel-/ Leberspätzle-suppe (A)	*lehbuhknerdel-/ lehbuhschpet-zluhzuppuh*	Consommé with liver dumplings
Grießnockerl-suppe (A)	*greesnokerlzuppuh*	Consommé with semolina dumplings
Tiroler Speckknödel-suppe (A)	*Tiroller shpek-knerdelzoope*	Consommé with bacon dumplings

Currywurst mit Pommes

Curry-flavoured sausage certainly isn't gourmet, but it's a must-try. Originally from Berlin, this popular snack – served with chips – stars at **Würstchenbuden** (sausage stands) all over the region.

Second course dishes

Nürnberger Rostbratwürste	*nyurnberguh rosst-braatvuerstuh*	Typical Nuremberg fried sausages
Königsberger Klöpse	*kernigsberguh klerpsuh*	Königsberg meat dumplings
Gemüse-/ Fleischstrudel	*gemuesuh-/ flyschstroodel*	Vegetable or meat strudel
Matjesfilet mit Äpfeln und Kartoffeln	*maatjesfillet mit epfeln unt kartoffeln*	Herring fillet with apples and potatoes
Hering mit Pellkartoffeln	*hehring mit pellkartoffeln*	Herring with boiled potatoes
Schollenfilet mit Kartoffelsalat	*schollenfillet mit kartoffelsalaat*	Fillet of plaice and potato salad
Weißkohlpudding	*vicekohlpudding*	Cabbage and meat pudding
Rindsroulade	*rintsroollaaduh*	Beef roulade
Schweinsmedaillons	*schvynssmehdaalyohns*	Pork medallions
Kalbsleber	*kalbslehber*	Calf's liver
Gebackenes Schnitzel	*guhbackenuhs schnitzel*	Breaded veal or pork cutlet
Jägerschnitzel	*yaeguhschnitzel*	Cutlet with gravy and mushrooms
Zigeunerschnitzel	*tsigoynuhschnitzel*	Cutlet with spicy vegetables
Cordon Bleu	*cordon bleu*	Breaded meat with ham and cheese
Gulasch mit Knödeln, Nudeln oder Spätzle	*goulash mit knerdeln, noodeln oder spetzluh*	Goulash with tiny dough dumplings, pasta or noodles
Entenbrust	*entenbrust*	Duck breast
Hirschragout mit Preiselbeeren	*hirshragoo mit pryzelbearen*	Venison stew with cranberries
Hirschrücken/ Rehrücken (mit Spätzle und Pilzen)	*hirshruecken/rehruecken (mit spetzluh unt pilzen)*	Rack of venison (with tiny noodles and mushrooms)
Wildschweinbraten mit Klößen	*viltschvinebraaten mit klerssen*	Wild boar roast with dumplings
Schinkenfleckerl/ Krautfleckerl (A)	*shinkenflekurl/ krautflekurl*	Pasta dish with ham or cabbage
Speckknödel/ Fleischknödel (A)	*shpekknerdel/ fliyshknerdel*	Dumplings filled with meat or bacon

Kärntner Kasnudeln (A)	kerntnuh karznoodeln	Pasta with a potato and curd filling
Bündner Rösti (CH)	boondnuh rooshdi	Rösti with bacon, cheese, fried egg
Berner Platte (CH)	bernuh plattuh	Meats, sausages, potatoes and beans
Chäswaie (CH)	kayzvyuh	Pastry with cheese, egg and milk filling

Side dishes

Sauerkraut	zowuhkrowt	Pickled cabbage
Rotkraut	rohtkrowt	Red cabbage
Kartoffelbrei	kartoffelbry	Mashed potatoes
Bratkartoffeln	braatkartoffeln	Fried potatoes
Pommes Frites	pommuhs freets	Chips
Rösti	rooshdi	Grated fried potato
Knödel/Klöße	knerdel/klerssuh	Dumplings
Nudeln	noodeln	Noodles
Spätzle	spetzluh	Gnocchi-like noodles
Reis	rice	Rice

Desserts

Apfelstrudel	apfelstroodel	Apple strudel
Apfelküchle	apfelkooshluh	Apple cake
Gemischtes Eis	guhmishtuhs ice	Mixed ice cream
Bananensplit	banaanenschpilt	Banana, ice cream and choc sauce
Rote Grütze mit Sahne oder Vanillesauce	rohtuh gruetzuh mit zahnuh oduh vanilluhzorsuh	Red berry jelly with whipped cream or vanilla sauce
Bayerische Creme	byuhrishuh crem	Egg, milk and sugar pudding
Welfenspeise	velfenschpysuh	Vanilla-flavoured whipped egg white

Popular sweets, cakes & tarts

Schwarzwälder Kirschtorte	schvaarzvelduh kirschtortuh	Black Forest gateau
Friesentorte	freezentortuh	Cake with cream and plum puree
Quarkkuchen	qvarkkoochen	Curd cheesecake
Schmandkuchen	schmantkoochen	Sweet bread with fruit and cream

Stollen	_schtollen_	Christmas bread, dried fruits and nuts
Krapfen/Berliner	_Krapfen/berleenuh_	Filled doughnuts
Pflaumenknödel	_pflowmenknerdel_	Quark dumplings filled with plums
Süße Knödel (A)	_zuesse knerdel_	Sweet, hot, fruit-filled dumplings
Germknödel (A)	_gaymknerdel_	Dumpling with plum jam, poppy seeds and sugar on top
Sachertorte (A)	_zakhuhtortuh_	Chocolate cake with apricot jam
Salzburger Nockerln (A)	_zalzburghuh nokerln_	Sweet soufflé
Zuger Kirschtorte (CH)	_tsooguh kearshtortuh_	Cream and cherry schnapps tart
Rüblitorte (CH)	_roobleytortuh_	Carrot cake
Basler Leckerli (CH)	_bazluh lekerley_	Ginger biscuits
Vermicelles (CH)	_vermitchelles_	Chestnut paste

Wheat beer

In most parts of Bavaria, the wheat beer is called **Weißbier**. Served in special glasses, it's sometimes topped with a lemon slice. The **Weizenbock** has a higher alcohol content.

Drinks

Kaffee mit Milch	_caffay mit milkh_	Coffee with milk
Schwarzer Kaffee	_schvaarzuh kaffay_	Black coffee
Pharisäer	_faareezayuh_	Coffee, rum and whipped cream
Rüdesheimer Kaffee	_rueduhshymuh caffay_	Coffee with flambéed brandy
Heiße Schokolade	_highsuh schockolaaduh_	Hot chocolate

Koffeinfreier Kaffee (mit milch)	*koffeenfryuh caffay (mit milkh)*	Decaffeinated coffee (with milk)
Schwartee (mit Milch/Zitrone)	*schvaartay (mit milkh/tsitrohnuh)*	Tea (with milk/lemon)
Früchte-/Kräutertee	*frueschtuh-/kroytuhtay*	Fruit/herbal tea
Eiskaffee	*icecaffay*	Iced coffee with vanilla ice cream
Mineralwasser (mit/ohne Gas)	*mineraalvassuh (mit/ohnuh gaaz)*	Still/sparkling mineral water
Orangensaft	*ohraanjenzaaft*	Orange juice
Apfelsaft	*apfelzaaft*	Apple juice
Apfelsaftschorle	*apfelzaaftschorluh*	Apple juice, soda
Limonade	*limonaaduh*	Lemonade
Cola	*cohla*	Coke
Radler	*raadluh*	Shandy
Bier (vom Fass)	*beeuh (fom fass)*	Beer (draught)
Weizenbier	*vyzenbeeuh*	Wheat beer
Rot-/ Weiß-/ Roséwein	*roht-/vice-/rohsayvine*	Red/white/rosé wine

Snacks

Currywurst	*curryvorst*	Sliced sausage with curry powder
Pommes mit Majo und Ketchup	*pommuhs mit mahyo unt ketchup*	Chips with mayo and ketchup
Leberkäse	*lehbuhkaysuh*	Minced meat loaf, usually in a roll
Döner kebab	*dernuh kebab*	Meat in a pita with onions, sauce, etc.

Another delicacy

A **Spanferkel** is a whole young pig with a crunchy skin, best grilled on charcoal. A typical way to serve it is with bread dumplings, and red or white cabbage.

Shopping

Probably no other region blends shopping and countryside tours quite so effortlessly. The Crystal Road in Eastern Bavaria and the Porcelain Road in Thuringia are the best examples of this excellent mix.

Historic centres – often pedestrianised – are ideal places for strolling, looking and – why not? – buying a little something for back home. Whenever possible, visit one of the big flea markets. Not only are they colourful, but also they're often open on Sundays, when other shops usually remain closed.

Germany, Austria and Switzerland are streets ahead when it comes to organic and home-grown produce, too. Visit local markets for honey, crafts and **schnapps** (fruit brandy).

29

Essentials

Where can I buy...?	**Wo kann ich... kaufen?**	*vo kann ish... cowfen?*
Do you sell...?	**Verkaufen Sie...?**	*fercowfen zee...?*
I'd like this	**Ich hätte das gerne**	*ish hettuh dass gernuh*
I'd prefer...	**Ich bevorzuge...**	*ish buhfortsuguh...*
Could you show me...?	**Könnten Sie mir... zeigen?**	*kernten zee mihr... tsighgen?*
I'm just looking, thanks	**Ich schau mich nur um, danke**	*ish schow mish nur um, dankuh*
How much is it?	**Wieviel kostet das?**	*veefeel kostet dass?*
Could you write down the price?	**Könnten Sie den Preis aufschreiben?**	*kernten zee deign price owfschryben?*
Do you have any items on sale?	**Gibt es irgendetwas im Ausverkauf?**	*geebt ez ihrgentetvass im ausfercowf?*
Nothing else, thanks	**Das ist alles, danke**	*dass isst alluhs, dankuh*
Do you accept credit cards?	**Akzeptieren Sie Kreditkarten?**	*actsepteeren zee kraydeetkarten?*
Could you post it to...?	**Könnten Sie es an... schicken?**	*kernten zee ez an... schicken?*
Can I exchange it?	**Kann ich es umtauschen?**	*kann ish ez umtowschen?*
I'd like to return this	**Ich würde das gerne zurückgeben**	*ish vurduh dass gernuh tsurueckgehben*
I'd like a refund	**Ich hätte gerne eine Rückvergütung**	*ish hettuh gernuh eyenuh rueckferguetung*

Local specialities

From a Swiss cuckoo clock to a Christmas pyramid from the Ore Mountains, handcrafted products reflect the heritage of each region. Most have one thing in common, though: that legendary quality. Popular souvenirs are an original piece of the fallen Berlin Wall, symbol of the country's reunification, or Sachertorte from Vienna's Hotel Sacher.

The world's best cutlery

Solingen, a town in North Rhine-Westphalia, is primarily associated with one thing: sharp knives. Most department stores stock these blades and cutlery at quite good prices.

Can you recommend a shop selling local specialities?	**Können Sie mir ein Geschäft empfehlen, das lokale Spezialitäten verkauft?**	*kernen zee mihr eyn guhschaeft empfehlen, dass lokaaluh spetsiaali-taeten ferkowft?*
What are the local specialities?	**Welches sind die lokalen Spezialitäten?**	*velchuhs zind dee lokaalen spetsiaali-taeten?*
Is... (leather) good quality?	**Ist... (das Leder) von guter Qualität?**	*isst... (dass lehduh) fon gootuh qvali-taet?*
Is it hand made?	**Ist das handgearbeitet?**	*isst dass hantguhar-beitet?*
Do you make it to measure?	**Machen Sie auch Maß anfertigungen?**	*makhen zee owkch mass anfertigungen?*
Can I order one?	**Kann ich eine/ n/s bestellen?**	*kann ish eyenuh/ un/uhs beschtellen?*

Popular things to buy

Meissner Porzellan	*micenuh portsel-laan*	Meissen porcelain
Porzellanfiguren von Volkstedt-Rudolstadt	*portsellaanfigooren fon folkschtedt-roodolschadt*	Handmade painted porcelain figurines from Volkstedt
Kristallgläser aus Zwiesel	*kristaalglaesuh owss tsveezel*	Crystal glasses from Zwiesel

Lauschaer Christbaumschmuck	*lowscher cristbowmschmuck*	Glass Christmas tree ornaments from Lauscha
Bierkrug aus Steingut oder Keramik	*beerkroog ows schtighngoot oduh keraamik*	Traditional ceramic or stoneware German beer jugs
Trachten (Dirndl, Lederhose, Hut)	*traakhten (dirndul, lehduhhohsuh, hoot)*	Typical Bavarian dirndls, leather shorts, hats
Schwarzwalduhren	*schvaartsvaltuhren*	Handcrafted Black Forest clogs
Holzschnitzereien aus dem Erzgebirge	*holzschnittserigen ows dame ertzguhbeerguh*	Wood carvings from the Ore Mountains
Plauener Spitzen und Stickereien	*plowenuh schpitzen unt schtickuhrigen*	Plauen lace and embroidery (Saxony)
Berliner Mauerstein	*berleenuh mowuhsschtighn*	Original piece of the Berlin Wall
Produkte mit dem Ampelmann	*prohduktuh mit dame ampelman*	Ampelmann (traffic-light man) products
Nürnberger Lebkuchen	*nuernberguh lehbkoohen*	Gingerbread biscuits from Nuremberg
Lübecker Marzipan	*luebeckuh martsipan*	Marzipan from Lübeck
Weine	*vyssvynuh*	Wines
Schokolade	*shokolarde*	Chocolate
Schweizer Uhren	*shviytser oaren*	Swiss watches
Steirisches Kürbiskernöl	*shtiyrishes kurbiskernerl*	Pumpkin seed oil from Styria
Raclettegrill	*rakletgrill*	Grill for raclette

Food for the gods

Switzerland's chocolate-making tradition was started in 1819 by François-Louis Cailler, who learnt his craft in Turin. The factory he established in Vevey still produces Cailler chocolate to this day.

Christmas the whole year round

Compiling your wish-list and dreaming of decorating the tree in July? No problem. The famous Käthe Wohlfahrt Christmas shop in Rothenburg opens its doors the whole year round.

Clothes & shoes

The small town of Metzingen near Stuttgart in Baden-Württemberg is attracting bargain shoppers from all over Europe. Hugo Boss was the first designer to open a factory outlet here, selling his clothes, shoes and accessories at reasonable prices. Other labels such as Joop, Escada, Bogner and Jil Sander followed his example.

Where is the... department?	**Wo ist die... abteilung?**	vo isst dee...aptyeloong?
- clothes	**- Kleider-**	- klyduh-
- shoe	**- Schuh-**	- schooh-
- women's	**- Damen-**	- dahmen-
- men's	**- Herren-**	- herren-
- children's	**- Kinder-**	- kinduh-
I'm looking for...	**Ich suche...**	ish zoochuh...
- a skirt	**- einen Rock**	- eyenen rock
- trousers	**- eine Hose**	- eyenuh hohsuh
- a top	**- ein Oberteil**	- eyn ohbuhtile
- a jacket	**- ein Jackett**	- eyn jahkett
- a T-shirt	**- ein T-Shirt**	- eyn tee-shirt
- jeans	**- eine Jeans**	- eyenuh jeans
- shoes	**- Schuhe**	- schoohuh
- underwear	**- Unterwäsche**	- unterveshchuh
Can I try it on?	**Kann ich es anprobieren?**	kann ish ez anprhbeeren?
What size is it?	**Welche Größe ist das?**	velchuh grurssuh isst dass?

A royal avenue

Düsseldorf is Germany's fashion capital and the **Königsallee** – or **Kö**, as the locals say affectionately – is the city's noblest street. Don't dally here without a platinum credit card in your pocket.

My size is...	**Meine Größe ist...**	_mynuh grurssuh isst..._
- small	**- Small**	_- schmall_
- medium	**- Medium**	_- maydeeum_
- large	**- Large**	_- large_

(see clothes size converter on p.96 for full range of sizes)

Do you have this in my size?	**Haben Sie das in meiner Größe?**	_hahben zee dass in mynuh grurssuh?_
Where is the changing room?	**Wo ist die Umkleidekabine?**	_vo isst dee umkly-duhkabeenuh?_

It doesn't fit	**Es passt nicht**	_ez passt nikht_
It doesn't suit me	**Es steht mir nicht**	_ez stayht mihr nikht_
Do you have a... size?	**Haben Sie eine... Größe?**	_hahben zee eyenuh grurssuh?_
- bigger	**- größere**	_- grurssuhruh_
- smaller	**- kleinere**	_- klynuhruh_

Do you have it/them in...	**Haben Sie es/sie in...**	_hahben zee ez/zee in..._
- black?	**- schwarz?**	_- schvarz?_
- white?	**- weiß?**	_- vice?_
- blue?	**- blau?**	_- blouh?_
- green?	**- grün?**	_- gruehn?_
- red?	**- rot?**	_- roht?_

I'm going to leave it/them	**Ich nehme es/sie nicht**	*ish nehmuh ez/zee nikht*
I'll take it/them	**Ich nehme es/sie**	*ish nehmuh ez/zee*

You may hear...

Kann ich Ihnen helfen?	*kann ish eenen helfen?*	Can I help you?
Welche Größe?	*velchuh grurssuh?*	What size?
Wir haben gar keine	*vihr hahben gar kynuh*	We don't have any
Hier bitte sehr	*heeuh bittuh zehr*	Here you are
Noch etwas, bitte?	*nokh etvass, bittuh?*	Anything else?
Soll ich es Ihnen einpacken?	*zoll ish ez eenen eynpacken?*	Shall I wrap it for you?
Das macht... (50) Euro	*dass makht... (fuenftsig) oyroh*	It's... (50) euros
Es ist reduziert	*ez isst redutseeert*	It's reduced

Where to shop

Where can I find...	**Wo gibt es...**	*vo geebt ez...*
- a bookshop?	**- einen Buchladen?**	*- eyenen boochlaaden?*
- a clothes shop?	**- ein Kleidergeschäft?**	*- eyn klyduhguh-schaeft?*
- a department store?	**- ein Kaufhaus?**	*eyn kowfhowss?*
- a gift shop?	**- einen Geschen-kartikelladen?**	*- eyenen guhschen-kkarteekelaaden?*
- a music shop?	**- ein Musikgeschäft?**	*- eyn mooseekguh-schaeft?*
- a market?	**- einen Markt?**	*- eyenen markt?*

Button in the ear

Margarete **Steiff** began producing exquisite teddy bears in 1902. Admire these heirloom toys and other plush animals at the company's museum, conveniently near the factory outlet in Giengen, southwest Germany.

35

- a newsagent?	- einen Zeitschrift- enladen?	- _eyenen tsightschrift- enlaaden?_
What's the best place to buy...?	**Wo kauft man am besten...?**	_vo kowft man am besten...?_
I'd like to buy...	**Ich würde gerne... kaufen**	_ich vuerde gernuh... cowfen_
- a film	- **einen Film**	- _eyenen feelm_
- an English newspaper	- **eine englische Zeitung**	- _eyenuh ennglis- shuh tsightung_
- a map	- **einen Stadtplan**	- _eyenen schtadtplan_
- postcards	- **Postkarten**	- _posstkarten_

Food & markets

Is there a supermarket/ market nearby?	**Gibt es in der Nähe einen Super- markt/Markt?**	_geebt ez in der naehuh eyenen zoopermarkt/markt?_
Can I have...	**Kann ich... haben?**	_kann ish... hahben?_
- some bread?	- **Brot**	- _broht_
- some fruit?	- **Früchte**	- _frueschtuh_
- some cheese?	- **Käse**	- _kaysuh_
- a bottle of water/wine?	- **eine Flasche Wasser/Wein**	- _eyenuh flaschuh vassuh/vine_
I'd like... of that	**Ich hätte gerne... davon**	_ish hettuh gernuh... dafon_
- half a kilo	- **ein halbes Kilo**	- _eyn halbuhs keeloh_
- 250 grams	- **250 Gramm**	- _tsivgh hundrert fuenftsig gram_

Department store of the West

The **Kaufhaus des Westens – KaDeWe** for short – opened in 1907. Today it's a must for all visitors to Berlin, especially for the **Feinschmeckeretage**, the world's largest gourmet food department.

Getting around

More than twenty airlines offer direct flights from the UK to various German, Austrian and Swiss cities. The Inter City Express (ICE) – the efficient high-speed train – conveniently links major German destinations, with some routes continuing to Austria and Switzerland.

The region's famous scenic routes are yet another way to explore the country. Follow the Brothers Grimm's footsteps on the Fairytale Route, pass historical towns and fairytale castles on the Romantic Road, explore snow-gilded peaks on the Alpine Road or taste the best local vintages on the Wine Road.

Arrival

Brits can reach Germany, Austria and Switzerland conveniently and quickly – and not only by air. Take a car ferry to Calais, Zeebrugge or Rotterdam, then drive south (just budget for expensive tolls on motorways outside Germany). Another alternative is the Eurostar. The international train service whizzes under the Channel and then links to many of the region's key cities.

Where is/are...	**Wo ist/sind...**	*vo isst/zint...*
- the luggage from flight...?	**- das Gepäck von Flug...?**	*- dass guh<u>peck</u> fon floog...?*
- the luggage trolleys?	**- die Gepäckwagen?**	*- dee guh<u>peck</u>vahgen?*
- the lost luggage office?	**- das Fundbüro?**	*- dass <u>funt</u>byuroh?*

Where is/are...	**Wo ist/sind...**	*vo isst/zint...*
- the buses?	**- die Busse?**	*- dee <u>bussuh</u>?*
- the trains?	**- die Züge?**	*- dee <u>tsueguh</u>?*
- the taxis?	**- Taxis?**	*- <u>taxees</u>?*
- the car rental?	**- ein Autoverleih?**	*- eyn <u>owtoeferligh</u>?*
- the exit?	**- der Ausgang?**	*- der <u>owssgang</u>?*
How do I get to hotel...?	**Wie gelange ich zum Hotel...?**	*vee guh<u>languh</u> ish tsoom hoh<u>tel</u>...?*

My baggage...	**Mein Gepäck...**	*mine guh<u>peck</u>...*
- is lost	**- ist verloren gegangen**	*- isst fer<u>lohren</u> guh<u>gangen</u>*
- is damaged	**- ist beschädigt**	*- isst buh<u>schaedigt</u>*
- is stolen	**- wurde gestohlen**	*- <u>vurduh</u> guh<u>schtohlen</u>*

Welcome cards

Many cities offer these cards for a small lump sum; they provide unlimited use of local transport. Moreover, the deal includes free or reduced admission to various tourist attractions.

Customs

Unlike citizens from Schengen countries, who are covered by one visa allowing uninterrupted travel to all member countries, Brits must show their passports when entering other EU countries. Be prepared for potential queues in the non-Schengen transit areas of airports, crowded with tourists from more remote locales. Also, remember that you can be subject to checks at any entrance point.

The children are on this passport	**Meine Kinder sind in diesem Pass eingetragen**	*mynuh kinder zint in deezem pass eynguhtraagen*
We're here on holiday	**Wir sind hier auf Urlaub**	*vihr zint heeuh owf uhrlowp*
I'm going to...	**Ich reise nach...**	*ish righsuh nakh...*
I have nothing to declare	**Ich habe nichts zu deklarieren**	*ish hahbuh nikhts tsue deklaareeren*
Do I have to declare this?	**Muss ich das deklarieren?**	*muss ish dass deklaareeren?*

Car hire

The big car rental firms here are international, so you can pre-book over the Internet. Their websites often offer online discounts. Airports and some train stations have auto-hire kiosks. Hotel receptionists can provide further contacts and information. Once you're behind the wheel, the autobahn is all yours.

I'd like to hire...	**Ich würde gerne... mieten**	*ish vuerduh gernuh... meeten*
- a car	**- ein Auto**	*- eyn owtoe*
- a people carrier	**- einen People Carrier**	*- eyenen people carrier*
with...	**mit...**	*mit...*
- air conditioning	**- Klimaanlage**	*- kleemahanlaaguh*
- automatic transmission	**- Automatik-getriebe**	*- owtoemaatik-guhtreebuh*
How much is that for a...	**Wieviel kostet das pro...**	*veefeel kostet dass proh...*
- day?	**- Tag?**	*- taag?*
- week?	**- Woche?**	*- vochuh?*
Does that include...	**Inkludiert das...**	*inkluediiert dass...*

- mileage?	**- freie Kilometer?**	*- fryuh keelomaytuh?*
- insurance?	**- die Versicherung?**	*- dee ferzishuhrung?*

High-speed motorways

The Germans do like it fast: their autobahns post no speed limits. The experience sometimes resembles a Formula One track – the excitement, chills and spills. Be careful!

On the road

Motoring enthusiasts adore Germany, with its modern and extensive road network. Motorways here are free, unlike in Austria and Switzerland, where vignette systems tap travellers' wallets. Service stations are frequent along the autobahns and provide drivers with varied services, including cafeterias, restaurants, conference rooms and even hotels.

What is the speed limit?	**Welches Tempolimit gilt hier?**	*vellchuhs tempohlimit guilt heeuh?*
Can I park here?	**Kann ich hier parken?**	*kann ish heeuh parken?*
Where is a petrol station?	**Wo gibt es eine Tankstelle?**	*vo geebt ez eyenuh tankschtelluh?*
Please fill up the tank with...	**Bitte füllen Sie den Tank mit...**	*bittuh fuellen zee deign tank mit...*
- unleaded	**- bleifreiem Benzin**	*- blyfryem bentseen*
- diesel	**- Diesel**	*- deezel*
- leaded	**- Bleibenzin**	*- blybetseen*
- LPG	**- Autogas**	*- owtoegaas*

Directions

Is this the road to...?	**Ist das die Straße nach...?**	*isst dass dee schtraassuh nakh...?*
How do I get to...?	**Wie komme ich zu/nach...?**	*vie kommuh ish tsue/nakh...?*
How far is it to...?	**Wie weit ist es bis/nach...?**	*vie vight isst ez bis/nakh...?*

How long will it take to...?	**Wie lange dauert es bis/nach...?**	*vee languh dowert ez biss/nakh...?*
Could you point it out on the map?	**Können Sie mir das auf der Karte zeigen?**	*kernen zee mihr dass owf der kartuh tsighgen?*
I've lost my way	**Ich habe mich verirrt**	*ish hahbuh mish ferihrt*
On the right/left	**Rechts/links**	*rekhts/links*
Turn right/left	**Biegen Sie nach rechts/links ab**	*beegen zee nakh rekhts/links app*
Straight ahead	**Geradeaus**	*geraaduhowss*
Turn around	**Wenden Sie**	*venden zee*

Public transport

Germany boasts one of the world's best public transport systems. Bigger cities have underground networks, smaller ones comprehensive bus and tram systems. The punctuality of the **Deutsche Bahn** is world-famous; with a **Länder-Ticket**, you can travel a federal state by rail for a whole day, paying an insignificant sum. Austria's and Switzerland's rail services are equally polished.

Bus	**Der Bus**	*der buss*
Bus station	**Der Busbahnhof**	*der bussbahnhohf*
Train	**Der Zug/die Bahn**	*der tsuug/dee bahn*
Train station	**Der Bahnhof**	*der bahnhohf*

I would like to go to...	**Ich möchte nach... fahren**	*ish merschtuh nakh... fahren*
I would like a... ticket	**Ich hätte gerne eine...**	*ish hettuh gernuh eyenuh...*
- single	**- einfache Fahrkahrte**	*- eynfakhuh fahrkartuh*
- return	**- Rückfahrkarte**	*- rueckfahrkartuh*
- first class	**- Fahrkarte für die erste Klasse**	*- fahrkartuh fuer dee erstuh klassuh*
- smoking/non-smoking	**- Fahrkarte im Raucherabteil/ Nichtraucherabteil**	*- fahrkartuh im rowkuhapptighl/ nikhtrowkuhapptighl*

| What time does it leave/arrive? | **Wann fährt er ab/kommt er an?** | *vann fert er app/kommt er an?* |
| Could you tell me when to get off? | **Können Sie mir sagen, wann ich aussteigen muss?** | *kernen zee mihr zaagen, vann ish owsstighgen muss?* |

Taxis

I'd like a taxi to...	**Ich hätte gerne ein Taxi nach...**	*ish hette gernuh eyn taxee nakh...*
How much is it to the...	**Wieviel kostet es bis...**	*veefeel kostet ez biss...*
- airport?	**- zum Flughafen?**	*- tsum flooghafen?*
- town centre?	**- ins Stadtzentrum?**	*- inss schtadttsentroom?*
- hotel?	**- ins Hotel?**	*- inss hohtel?*

Tours

One of the best excursions is a short river cruise through the romantic, vineyard-swathed hills along the Middle Rhine, passing beautiful medieval castles and exploring the Lorelei myth. Wonderful cycle tours also lead guests through this area (**oberes Mittelrheintal**), which UNESCO declared a World Heritage Site in 2002. Similar tours are available along the Danube in Austria and on Switzerland's lakes.

Are there any organised tours of the town/region?	**Gibt es geführte Touren durch die Stadt/Region?**	*geebt ez gefuertuh touren dorch dee schtadt/raygion?*
Where do they leave from?	**Wo starten sie?**	*vo schtarten zee?*
What time does it start?	**Wann starten sie?**	*vann schtarten zee?*
Do you have English-speaking guides?	**Haben Sie english-sprachige Führer?**	*hahben zee ennglish-schprachiguh fuehruh?*
Do we get any free time?	**Haben wir auch eine freie Zeit?**	*hahben vihr owkch eyenuh fryuh tsight?*
Is lunch/tea included?	**Ist das Mittagessen/eine Kaffeepause inbegriffen?**	*isst dass mit-taaggessen/eyenuh caffaypowsuh inbuhgriffen?*
Are we going to see...?	**Werden wir... besichtigen?**	*verden vihr... buhsishtigen?*
What time do we get back?	**Wann kommen wir zurück?**	*vann kommen vihr tsuerueck?*

Accommodation

Germany, Austria and Switzerland have grand hotels aplenty, but nature lovers are the real winners here. After a day's hiking or biking, rest your head in the comfort of a farmhouse or wine estate. These rural retreats make economical – and very charming – holiday settings. Around 800 hostels welcome travellers – both young and young at heart – and thousands of excellent campsites are a great budget option.

To splurge, take the waters at a spa resort. Complexes offer saunas, hot pools and treatments (medical and cosmetic). They're usually set in gracious, somewhat nostalgic, towns that offer pedalos, mini-golf, riverside beer gardens and free concerts in ornate park bandstands.

Types of accommodation

The region's accommodation varies as much as its landscape. Linger over cocktails in a chic metropolitan hotel lobby – Vienna's Imperial is star of the show. Or book hiking holidays in a cosy Black Forest home or in a Bavarian country house, set within a marvellous alpine panorama. Traditional country estates host equestrians in the former East German land Mecklenburg-West Pomerania.

I'd like to stay in...	Ich würde gerne... wohnen	ish _vuerduh_ _gernuh.._ _vohnen_
- an apartment	- in einem Apartment	- in _eyenem_ _apart_ment
- a campsite	- auf einem Campingplatz	- owf _eyenem_ _camp_ingplatz
- a hotel	- in einem Hotel	- in _eyenem_ _hohtel_
- an apart-hotel	- in einem Apart-Hotel	- in _eyenem_ _apart_hohtel
- a youth hostel	- in einer Jugendherberge	- in _eyenuh_ _yugentherberguh_
- a guest house	- in einem Gästehaus	- in _eyenem_ _gestuhhowss_
Is it...	Ist es...	isst es...
- full board?	- Vollpension?	- _follpunsiohn?_
- half board?	- Halbpension?	- _halppunsiohn?_
- self-catering?	- mit Selbstverpflegung?	- mit _zelbst_ferpflegung?

Comfort of the herring kings

North Germany's Hanseatic cities grew to power thanks to the fishing trade. Today they boast well-preserved historic centres, picturesque harbours and traditional inns, plus the famed **deutsche Gemütlichkeit** (German cosiness).

Reservations

Do you have any rooms available?	**Haben Sie Zimmer frei?**	*hahben zee tsimmuh fry?*
I'd like to make a reservation for...	**Ich würde gerne eine Reservierung für... machen**	*ish vuerduh gernuh eyenuh reserveerung fuer... makhen*
- tonight	**- heute Nacht**	*- hoytuh nakht*
- one night	**- eine Nacht**	*- eyenuh nakht*
- two nights	**- zwei Nächte**	*- tsvigh neschtuh*
- a week	**- eine Woche**	*- eyenuh vokhuh*
From... (May 1st) to... (May 8th)	**Vom... (1. Mai) bis zum... (8. Mai)**	*fom... (ersten my) bis tsum... (akhten my)*

Room types

Amenities usually include a minibar, satellite TV and telephone in any hotel rated three stars or more. Laundry and dry cleaning are charged on top. More sophisticated, high-end properties may offer fitness rooms, saunas, booking agencies, business centres, meeting facilities, babysitting, wireless Internet and other services.

Do you have... room?	**Haben Sie ein... zimmer?**	*hahben zee eyn... tsimmuh?*
- a single	**- Einzel-**	*- eintsel-*
- a double	**- Doppel-**	*- doppel-*
- a family	**- Familien-**	*- fameeleeen-*
with...	**mit...**	*mit...*
- a cot?	**- Kinderbett?**	*- kinderbett?*
- twin beds?	**- zwei Einzelbetten?**	*- tsvigh eintselbetten?*
- a double bed?	**- einem Doppelbett?**	*- eyenem doppelbett?*
- a bath/shower?	**- Bad/Dusche?**	*- baad/duschuh?*
- air conditioning?	**- Klimaanlage?**	*- kleemaanlaaguh?*
- Internet access?	**- Internetzugang?**	*- internettsugang?*
Can I see the room?	**Kann ich das Zimmer sehen?**	*kann ish dass tsimmuh zehen?*

Prices

The rates for hotel rooms typically include taxes and breakfast – ask or scan for the line **inklusive Frühstück**. However, it's best to double check about other meals. Tipping is not obligatory, but it's expected from satisfied customers. Most hotel patrons give a euro or two per bag to hotel porters.

How much is...	**Wieviel kostet...**	_veefeel kostet..._
- a double room?	**- ein Doppelzimmer?**	_- eyn doppeltsimmuh?_
- per night?	**- es pro Nacht?**	_- ez pro nakht?_
- per week?	**- es pro Woche?**	_- ez pro vokhhuh?_
Is breakfast included?	**Ist das Frühstück inkludiert?**	_isst dass fruehschtuec inkloodeeert?_
Do you have...	**Gibt es...**	_geebt ez..._
- a reduction for children?	**- einen Rabatt für Kinder?**	_- eyenen rabaat fuer kinder?_
- a single room supplement?	**- einen Einzelzimmer-zuschlag?**	_- eyenen eintseltsimmuh-tsuschlaag?_
Is there...	**Gibt es...**	_geebt ez..._
- a swimming pool?	**- ein Schwimmbad?**	_- eyn schvimmbaad?_
- a lift?	**- einen Fahrstuhl?**	_- eyenen fahrschtoo_

For water babies

Popular holiday resorts lie on Germany's North and the Baltic Sea coasts, as well as along Lake Constance. Austria and Switzerland are of course famed for their watery escapes – try Lakes Geneva, Lucerne and Wörth.

Bett & Frühstück
Bed-and-breakfasts are also a popular and affordable way to spend holidays in German-speaking countries. Seek out a **Bett und Frühstück** or a less elaborate **Zimmer** (room).

I'll take it	**Ich nehme es**	*ish nehmuh ez*
Can I pay by...	**Kann ich mit...**	*kann ish mit...*
	bezahlen	*buhtsaahlen*
- credit card?	**- Kreditkarte?**	*- kraydeetkartuh?*
- traveller's cheques?	**- Reiseschecks?**	*- righsuhschecks?*

Special requests

Could you...	**Könnten Sie...**	*kernten zee...*
- put this in the hotel safe?	**- das in den Hotelsafe geben?**	*- dass in deign hohtelsafe gehben?*
- order a taxi for me?	**- ein Taxi für mich bestellen?**	*- eyn taxee fuer mikh beschtellen?*
- wake me up at (7am)?	**- mich um (7 Uhr früh) aufwecken?**	*- mikh um (zeeben uhr frueh) owfvecken?*
Is there...	**Gibt es...**	*geebt ez...*
- a safe?	**- einen Safe?**	*- eyenen safe?*
- a babysitting service?	**- einen Babysitterdienst?**	*- eyenen babysitterdeenst?*
- a laundry service?	**- einen Wäsche-Service?**	*- eyenen vaeschhuhserveecesuh?*
Is there wheelchair access?	**Gibt es einen Rollstuhlzugang?**	*geebt ez eyenen rohlschtooltsugang?*

47

Checking in & out

I have a reservation for tonight	**Ich habe eine Reservierung für heute Nacht**	*ish hahbuh eyenuh reserveerung fuer hoytuh nakht*
In the name of...	**Auf den Namen...**	*owf deign nahmen...*
Here's my passport	**Hier ist mein Reisepass**	*heeuh isst mine righsuhpass*
What time is check out?	**Wann muss ich auschecken?**	*vann muss ish owsschecken?*
Can I leave my bags here?	**Kann ich meine Reisetaschen hier lassen?**	*kann ish mynuh righsuhtaschen heeuh lassen?*
I'd like to check out	**Ich möchte gerne auschecken**	*ish merschtuh gernuh owsschecken*
Can I have the bill?	**Kann ich die Rechnung haben?**	*kann ish dee reshnung hahben?*

Camping

Do you have...	**Haben Sie...**	*hahben zee...*
- a site available?	**- einen Stellplatz verfügbar?**	*- eyenen schtellplatz ferfuegbar?*
- electricity?	**- Stromanschluss?**	*- schtromanschluss?*
- hot showers?	**- heiße Duschen?**	*- highsuh dooschen?*
- tents for hire?	**- Zelte zu mieten?**	*- tseltuh tsu meeten?*
How much is it per...	**Wieviel kostet es pro...**	*veefeel kostet ez pro...*
- tent?	**- Zelt?**	*- tselt?*
- caravan?	**- Wohnwagen?**	*- vohnvahgen?*
- person?	**- Person?**	*- perzohn?*
- car?	**- Wagen?**	*- vahgen?*
Where is/are the...	**Wo ist/sind die...**	*vo isst/zint dee...*
- reception?	**- Rezeption?**	*- retseptiohn?*
- bathrooms?	**- Waschräume?**	*- vashroymuh?*
- laundry facilities?	**- Waschmöglichkeiten?**	*- vaschmerglishkyten?*

Survival guide

Now part of the EU, Germany has replaced the Deutschmark and Austria the Schilling with the euro. Switzerland remains independent and uses Francs. Major credit cards can be used without problem. Note that small shops and companies may not accept them as widely as British businesses do.

At any bank in Germany, you'll encounter **Deutsche Gründlichkeit** (Teutonic thoroughness). You can expect the same virtue from the Deutsche Post. The digital culture is a bit more relaxed: enjoy a snack, coffee or cocktail, as you stay connected at an Internet café.

Money & banks

Where is the nearest...	Wo ist die/der/das nächste...	vo isst dee/der/dass naekhstuh...
- bank?	- Bank?	- bank?
- ATM/bank machine?	- Geldautomat?	- geltowtoemaat?
- foreign exchange office?	- Wechselbüro?	- vechselbyuro?
I'd like to...	Ich möchte...	ish merschte...
- withdraw money	- Geld abheben	- gelt apphehben
- cash a traveller's cheque	- einen Reisescheck einlösen	- eyenen righsuh- scheck eynlerzen
- change money	- Geld wechseln	- gelt vechseln
- arrange a transfer	- eine Überweisung durchführen	- eyenuh ooberveizung dorchfuehren
What's the exchange rate?	Wie steht der Wechselkurs?	vie stayht der vech- selcause?
What's the commission?	Wie hoch ist die Kommission?	vie hohkh isst dee kommissiohn?
What's the charge for...	Wie hoch sind die Gebühren für...	vee hohkh zind dee gebuerhren fuer...
- making a withdrawal?	- eine Geldabhebung?	- eyenuh geltapphehbung?
- exchanging money?	- Geld wechseln?	- gelt vechseln?
- cashing a cheque?	- das Einlösen eines Schecks?	- dass eyenlerzen eyenuhs schecks?
This is not right	Das stimmt nicht	dass schtimmt nikht
Is there a problem with my account?	Gibt es ein Problem mit meinem Konto?	geebt ez eyn pro- hblehm mit mynem kontoh?
The ATM/bank machine took my card	Der Geldautomat hat meine Karte eingezogen	der geltowtoemaat hat mynuh kartuh eynguhzohgen
I've forgotten my PIN	Ich habe meinen PIN-Code vergessen	ish hahbuh mynen pin-code fergessen

Post office

Where is the (main) post office?	**Wo ist das (Haupt-) Postamt?**	*vo isst dass (howpt-) posstamt?*
I'd like to send a...	**Ich möchte... senden**	*ish merschtuh... zenden*
- letter	**- einen Brief**	*- eyenen breef*
- postcard	**- eine Postkarte**	*- eyenuh posstkartuh*
- parcel	**- ein Paket**	*- eyn pakate*
- fax	**- ein Fax**	*- eyn fax*
I'd like to send this...	**Ich möchte das... senden**	*ish merschtuh dass... zenden*
- to the United Kingdom	**- ins Vereinigte Königreich**	*- inss fereynigtuh kernigrych*
- by airmail	**- per Luftpost**	*- per luftposst*
- by express mail	**- per Expresspost**	*- per expressposst*
- by registered mail	**- als Einschreiben**	*- alss eynschryben*
I'd like a stamp for this letter/ postcard	**Ich hätte gerne eine (Brief-) Marke für diesen Brief/für diese Postkarte**	*ish hette gernuh eyenuh (breef-) markuh fuer deezen breef/fuer deeze posstkartuh*
It's fragile	**Es ist zerbrechlich**	*ez isst tsehrbrekhlikh*

Prepaid SIM cards

Save on UK mobile roaming charges by using a local SIM card while away. Local calls and text messages are cheap; incoming calls free. Buy prepaid SIMs at post offices and local network providers.

Telecoms

Where can I make an international phone call?	**Wo kann ich ein Telefongespräch ins Ausland führen?**	*vo kann ish eyn telefohngespraech inss owsslant fuehren?*

Where can I buy a phonecard?	**Wo kann ich eine Telefonkarte kaufen?**	*vo kann ish eyenuh telefohnkartuh cowfen?*
How do I call abroad?	**Wie kann ich ins Ausland anrufen?**	*vie kann ish inss owsslant anroofen?*
How much does it cost per minute?	**Wieviel kostet es pro Minute?**	*veefeel kostet ez proh minootuh?*
The number is...	**Die Nummer lautet...**	*dee nummuh loutet...*
What's the area/country code for...?	**Wie lautet die Regionalkennzahl /Landeskennzahl für...?**	*vee loutet dee ray-giohnaalkenntsahl/ llanduhskenntsahl fuer...?*
The number is engaged	**Die Nummer ist besetzt**	*dee nummuh isst buhsetst*
The connection is bad	**Die Verbindung ist schlecht**	*dee ferbindung isst schlecht*
I've been cut off	**Die Leitung wurde unterbrochen**	*dee lytung vurduh unterbrokhen*
I'd like...	**Ich hätte gerne...**	*ish hettuh gernuh...*
- a charger for my mobile phone	**- ein Ladegerät für mein Mobiltelefon**	*- eyn laaduhgerate fuer mine mobeeltelefohn*
- an adaptor plug	**- einen Stecker für meinen Adapter**	*- eyenen schteckuh fuer mynen adaptuh*
- a pre-paid SIM card	**- eine SIM-Karte mit Guthaben**	*- eyenuh sim-kartuh mit goothahben*

Internet

Where's the nearest Internet café?	**Wo ist das nächste Internetcafé?**	*voh isst dass naech-stuh internetcafay?*
I'd like to...	**Ich würde gerne...**	*ish vuerduh gernuh...*
- use the Internet	**- das Internet benutzen**	*- dass internet benutzen*
- check my email	**- meine E-mail abrufen**	*- mynuh e-mail approofen*
- use a printer	**- einen Drucker benutzen**	*- eyenen druckuh benutzen*
How much is it...	**Wieviel kostet es...**	*veefeel kostet ez...*
- per minute?	**- pro Minute?**	*- proh minootuh?*
- per hour?	**- pro Stunde?**	*- proh schtunduh?*

- to buy a CD?	**- eine CD zu kaufen?**	*- eyenuh sayday tsu cowfen?*
How do I...	**Wie kann ich...**	*vee kann ish...*
- log on?	**- mich anmelden?**	*- mish anmelden?*
- open a browser?	**- einen Browser öffnen?**	*- eyenen browser erfnen?*
- print this?	**- das ausdrucken?**	*- dass owssdrucken?*
I need help with this computer	**Ich brauche Hilfe mit diesem Computer**	*ish browkuh hillfuh mit deezem computer*
The computer has crashed	**Der Computer ist abgestürzt**	*der compooter isst appguhschtuerzt*
I've finished	**Ich habe es beendet**	*ish hahbuh ez buhendet*

Pharmacies

Pharmacies in German-speaking Europe are reminiscent of old-fashioned apothecaries, with a more holistic and herbal tradition than in the UK.

Chemist

Where's the nearest (all-night) pharmacy?	**Wo ist die nächste Apotheke (mit Nachtdienst)?**	*vo isst dee naechst-uh apohtehkuh (mit nakhtdeenst)?*
I need something for...	**Ich brauche etwas gegen...**	*ish browkuh etvass gehgen...*
- diarrhoea	**- Durchfall**	*- dorchfal*
- a cold	**- Erkältung**	*- erkeltung*
- a cough	**- Husten**	*- husten*
- sunburn	**- Sonnenbrand**	*- zonnenbrant*
- motion sickness	**- Reiseübelkeit**	*- rysuhoobelkite*
- hay fever	**- Heuschnupfen**	*- hoyschnupfen*
- period pain	**- Menstruations-schmerzen**	*- menstrooatiohns-schmerzen*

| - abdominal pains | - Bauchschmerzen | - _bowk_schmerzen |
| - a urine infection | - eine Blasen-entzündung | - _eyenuh_ _blahzen-_enttsuendung |

I'd like...	Ich hätte gerne...	ish _hettuh_ _gernuh_...
- aspirin	- Aspirin	- aspeereen
- plasters	- Pflaster	- _pflastuh_
- condoms	- Kondome	- kon_dohmuh_
- insect repellent	- Insekten-schutzmittel	- in_zekten_schutz_mitte_
- painkillers	- Schmerztabletten	- _schmerz_tabletten
- a contraceptive	- ein (Empfängnis-) Verhütungsmittel	- eyn (emp_fengnis_-) ver_hootungs_mittel

How much should I take?	Wieviel sollte ich davon nehmen?	vee_feel_ _zolltuh_ ish dafon _nehmen_?
Take...	Nehmen Sie...	_nehmen_ zee...
- a tablet	- eine Tablette	- _eyenuh_ tab_lettuh_
- a teaspoon	- einen Teelöffel voll	- _eyenen_ _tay_lerfel foll
- with water	- es mit Wasser	- ez mit _vassuh_

Is it suitable for children?	Ist es auch für Kinder geeignet?	isst ez owkh fuer _kinduh_ ge_eyegnet_?
Will it make me drowsy?	Macht es mich schläfrig?	makht ez mikh _schlaefrig_?
Do I need a prescription?	Brauche ich ein Rezept?	_brow_kuh ish eyn _retsept_?
I have a prescription	Ich habe ein Rezept	ish _hahbuh_ eyn _retsept_

Children

Where should I take the children?	Wohin könnte ich mit den Kindern gehen?	_vohin_ _kerntuh_ ish mit deign _kindern_ _gehen_?
Where is the nearest...	Wo ist der nächste...	vo isst der _naechstuh_...
- playground?	- Spielplatz?	- _schpeel_platz?
- fairground?	- Rummelplatz?	- _rummel_platz?
- zoo?	- Tierpark?	- _teer_park?
- park?	- Park?	- _park_?
Where is the nearest swimming pool?	Wo ist das nächste Schwimmbad?	vo isst dass _naechstuh_ _schvimm_baad?

Is this suitable for children?	Ist es für Kinder geeignet?	*isst ez fuer kinder geeyegnet?*
Are children allowed?	Sind Kinder zugelassen?	*zind kinder tsugelassen?*
Are there baby-changing facilities here?	Gibt es hier einen Wickelraum?	*geebt ez heeuh eyenen wickelrowm?*

Do you have...	Haben Sie...	*hahben zee...*
- a children's menu?	- eine Kinderspeisekarte?	*- eyenuh kinderschpysuhkartuh?*
- a high chair?	- einen Kinderhochstuhl?	*- eyenen kinderhokhschtoohl?*
Is there...	Gibt es...	*geebt ez...*
- a child-minding service?	- einen Babysitterdienst?	*- eyenen babysitterdeenst?*
- a nursery?	- eine Kinderkrippe?	*- eyenuh kinderkrippuh?*

I'd like to buy...	Ich möchte gerne... kaufen	*ish mershte gernuh... cowfen*
- nappies	- Windeln	*- vindeln*
- baby wipes	- Feuchttücher	*- foyschttueschuh*
- tissues	- Papiertaschentücher	*- papeertaschentueschuh*

An accessible country

Not only public transport is adapted for people with disabilities. An association in Hamburg organises cycle tours on tandems for blind people, while Berlin has a wheelchair breakdown service.

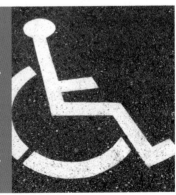

Travellers with disabilities

| I have a disability | Ich habe eine Behinderung | *ish hahbuh eyenuh buhinderung* |

I need assistance	**Ich brauche Unterstützung**	*ish browkhuh unterstuetzung*
I am blind	**Ich bin blind**	*ish bin blint*
I am deaf	**Ich bin schwerhörig/ taub**	*ish bin schvehrhoerig/towp*
I have a hearing aid	**Ich habe eine Hörhilfe**	*ish hahbuh eyenuh hoerhillfuh*
I can't walk well	**Ich kann nicht gut gehen**	*ish kann nikht goot gehen*
Is there a lift?	**Gibt es einen Fahrstuhl?**	*geebt ez eyenen faarschtool?*
Is there wheelchair access?	**Gibt es einen Rollstuhl-geeigneten Zugang?**	*geebt ez eyenen rohlschtoolgeeyegneten tsugang?*
Can I bring my guide dog?	**Kann ich meinen Blindenhund mitbringen?**	*kann ish mynen blindenhunt mitbringen?*
Are there disabled toilets?	**Gibt es Behinder-tentoiletten?**	*geebt ez buhhindertentwighletten?*
Do you offer disabled services?	**Bieten Sie Dienste für Behinderte an?**	*beeten zee deenstuh fuer buhhindertuh an?*
Could you help me...	**Könnten Sie mir dabei helfen...**	*kernten zee mihr dahbei helfen...*
- cross the street?	**- die Straße zu überqueren?**	*- dee schtraassuh tsu ooberqvehren?*
- go up/down the stairs?	**- die Treppe hoch/hinunter zu gehen?**	*- dee treppuh hokh/hinunter tsu gehen?*
Can I sit down somewhere?	**Kann ich mich irgendwo hinsetzen?**	*kann ish mikh ihrgentvo hinsetzten?*
Could you call a disabled taxi for me?	**Können Sie bitte ein Behinderten-taxi für mich rufen?**	*kernen zee bittuh eyn buhhindertentaxee fuer mikh roofen?*

Repairs & cleaning

This is broken	**Das ist kaputt**	*dass isst kaput*
Can you fix it?	**Können Sie es reparieren?**	*kernen zee ez repareeren?*

Do you have...	**Haben Sie...**	*hahben zee...*
- a battery?	**- eine Batterie?**	*- eyenuh batteree?*
- spare parts?	**- Ersatzteile?**	*- erzatztighluh?*
Can you... this?	**Können Sie das...**	*kernen zee dass...*
- clean	**- reinigen?**	*- rynigen?*
- press	**- bügeln?**	*- buegeln?*
- dry-clean	**- trocken reinigen?**	*- trocken rynigen?*
- patch	**- flicken?**	*- flicken?*
When will it be ready?	**Wann wird es fertig sein?**	*vann virt ez fertig zign?*
This isn't mine	**Das ist nicht meines**	*dass isst nikht mynuhs*

Meet me at the zoo

The Berlin Zoo is the oldest in Germany and has more species than any other zoo in the world. The aquarium leads visitors through colourful and impressive underwater worlds.

Tourist information

Where's the Tourist Information Office?	**Wo ist das Tourismusbüro?**	*vo isst dass tourizmuzbyuro?*
Do you have a city/regional map?	**Haben Sie einen Stadtplan/eine Regionalkarte?**	*hahben zee eyenen schadtpan/eyenuh rayghionaalkartuh?*
What are the main places of interest?	**Welches sind die wichtigsten Sehenswürdigkeiten?**	*velchuhs zint dee vishtigsten zehensvuerdigkighten?*
Could you show me on the map?	**Können Sie mir das bitte in der Karte zeigen?**	*kernen zee mihr dass bittuh in der kartuh tsighgen?*

Do you have a brochure in English?	**Haben Sie einen Prospekt in Englisch?**	*hahben zee eyenen prospect in ennglissh?*
We're interested in...	**Wir interessieren uns für...**	*vihr interresseerren unss fuer...*
- history	**- Geschichte**	*- geshishtuh*
- architecture	**- Architektur**	*- archeetektor*
- shopping	**- das Einkaufen**	*- dass eyncowfen*
- hiking	**- das Wandern**	*- dass vandern*
- a scenic walk	**- einen Aussich- tsrundgang**	*- eyenen owssihkts- untgang*
- a boat cruise	**- eine Bootsrundfahrt**	*- eyenuh boootsruntfaahrt*
- a guided tour	**- eine geführte Tour**	*- eyenuh gefuerhtuh tour*
Are there any excursions?	**Gibt es irgendwelche Exkursionen?**	*geebt ez ihrgentvelchuh exkurziohnen?*
How long does it take?	**Wie lange dauert es?**	*vee languh dowert es?*
What does it cost?	**Wieviel kostet das?**	*veefeel kostet dass?*
Are there any tours in English?	**Gibt es Touren auf Englisch?**	*geebt ez touren owf ennglissh?*

Get in shape with a city tour
Explore the sights in an unconventional way, for example on a bike. Or how does a sightseeing tour for joggers sound? In any case, don't forget your trainers!

Emergencies

Germany, Austria and Switerland are not dangerous countries, barring the odd pickpocket. Increased attention is appropriate at airports, railway stations and in crowded city centres. Remember to always carry a valid passport, as the police may ask for ID at any time. Don't assume medicine is free for EU citizens. The European Health Insurance Card (EHIC) only covers emergency treatment and private hospitals won't accept it. For this reason the UK Foreign Office recommends taking out travel insurance before departure.

Medical

Where is the...	Wo ist das...	*vo isst dass...*
- hospital?	- Krankenhaus?	*- krankenhowss?*
- health centre?	- Gesundheitszen-trum?	*- gezundhightstsen-trum?*

I need...	Ich brauche...	*ish browkuh...*
- a doctor	- einen Arzt	*- eyenen arzt*
- a female doctor	- eine Ärztin	*- eyenuh erztin*
- an ambulance	- einen Krankenwagen	*- eyenen krankenvahgen*
It's very urgent	Es ist sehr dringend	*ez isst zehr dringent*
I'm injured	Ich bin verletzt	*ish bin ferletzt*
I don't feel well	Ich fühle mich nicht gut	*ish fuehluh mish nihkt goot*

I have...	Ich habe...	*ish hahbuh...*
- a cold	- eine Erkältung	*- eyenuh erkeltung*
- diarrhoea	- Durchfall	*- dorchfal*
- a rash	- einen Ausschlag	*- eyenen owss-schlaag*
- a temperature	- erhöhte Temperatur	*- erhurtuh tempuhraator*

I have a lump here	Ich habe hier eine Geschwulst	*ish hahbuh heeuh eyenuh geschvulst*
Can I have the morning-after pill?	Kann ich die Pille danach haben?	*kann ish dee pilluh danakh hahben?*
It hurts here	Es tut mir hier weh	*ez toot mihr heeuh veigh*
How much do I owe you?	Wieviel schulde ich Ihnen?	*veefeel schullduh ish eenen?*
I have insurance	Ich bin versichert	*ish bin ferzishert*

Dentist

I need a dentist	Ich brauche einen Zahnarzt	*ish browkuh eyenen tsaahnarzt*
I have tooth ache	Ich habe Zahnschmerzen	*ish hahbuh tsaahnschmertsen*
My gums are swollen	Mein Zahnfleisch ist geschwollen	*mine tsaahnflysch isst guhschvollen*
This filling has fallen out	Diese Füllung ist herausgefallen	*deesuh fuellung isst herowssguhfalun*

I have an abscess	**Ich habe ein Abszess**	*ish hahbuh eyn abtsess*
I've broken a tooth	**Mir ist ein Zahn abgebrochen**	*mihr isst eyn tsaahn appguhbrochen*
Are you going to take it out?	**Werden Sie ihn herausnehmen?**	*verden zee een herowssnehmen?*

Crime

I want to report a theft	**Ich möchte einen Diebstahl melden**	*ish merchtuh eyenen deebschtaahl melden*
Someone has stolen my...	**Jemand hat... gestohlen**	*yaymant hat... geschtohlen*
- bag	**- meine Tasche**	*- mynuh tashhuh*
- car	**- mein Auto**	*- mine owtoe*
- credit cards	**- meine Kreditkarten**	*- mynuh kraydeetkarten*
- money	**- mein Geld**	*- mine gelt*
- passport	**- meinen Reisepass**	*- mynen righsuhpass*
I've been attacked	**Ich wurde überfallen**	*ish vurduh ueberfalun*

Always good to know

Just in case, there are two important numbers worth remembering: ring 110 for the police and 112 for the ambulance, fire brigade and other emergencies.

DIE JOHANNITER

Lost property

I've lost my...	**Ich habe... verloren**	*ish hahbuh... ferloren*
- car keys	**- meine Autoschlüssel**	*- mynuh owtoeschluessel*
- driving licence	**- meinen Führerschein**	*- mynen fuerhrerschine*

| - handbag | - **meine Handtasche** | - *mynuh hanttashuh* |
| - flight tickets | - **meine Flugtickets** | - *mynuh floogtickets* |

It happened...	**Es geschah...**	*ez guhschaah...*
- this morning	- **heute Morgen**	- *hoytuh morgen*
- today	- **heute**	- *hoytuh*
- in the hotel	- **im Hotel**	- *im hohtel*

Breakdowns

I've had...	**Ich hatte...**	*ish hattuh...*
- an accident	- **einen Unfall**	- *eyenen unfal*
- a breakdown	- **eine Panne**	- *eyenuh pannuh*
- a puncture	- **eine Reifenpanne**	- *eyenuh righfen-pannuh*

My battery is flat	**Meine Batterie ist leer**	*mynuh batteree isst lehr*
I don't have a spare tyre	**Ich habe keinen Ersatzreifen**	*ish hahbuh kynen ersatzrighfen*
I've run out of petrol	**Mir ist der Benzin ausgegangen**	*mihr isst der bentseen owss-guhgangen*
My car doesn't start	**Mein Wagen springt nicht an**	*mine vahgen sch-pringt nikht an*
Can you repair it?	**Können Sie es reparieren?**	*kernen zee ez repaareeren?*
I have breakdown cover	**Ich habe eine Pannen-versicherung**	*ish hahbuh eyenuh pannen-ferzishhuhrung*

Problems with the authorities

I'm sorry, I didn't realise...	**Es tut mir leid, mir war nicht bewusst, dass...**	*ez toot mihr light, mihr var nikht buhvusst, dass...*
- I was driving so fast	- **ich zu schnell fuhr**	- *ish tsue schnell fo*
- it was against the law	- **das gegen das Gesetz war**	- *dass gehgen dass gezetz var*

| Here are my documents | **Hier sind meine Fahrzeugpapiere** | *heeyuh zint mynuh faartsoygpapeeruh* |
| I'm innocent | **Ich bin unschuldig** | *ish bin unschuldig* |

Dictionary

The English-German dictionary in this chapter will help you formulate simple sentences, and the subsequent German-English one will rescue you when deciphering responses. In the German, we list nouns with their article: **der** for masculine, **die** for feminine and plural, **das** for neuter. If nouns can be either masculine or feminine, we display both: **Freund/in**, **der/die** (friend) means **der Freund** is a male friend (or boyfriend), **die Freundin** a female friend (or girlfriend). Finally, adjectives that form part of the noun, e.g. **Lieblingsbuch** for favourite book, have been denoted with a hyphen. For more tips on grammar and pronunciation, see the Introduction.

English-German dictionary

A

A&E	**Notaufnahme, die**	*nohtowfnaahmuh, dee*
a(n)	**ein/e**	*eyn/eyenuh*
about (concerning)	**über**	*ewber*
accident	**Unfall, der**	*unfal, der*
accommodation	**Unterkunft, die**	*unterkunft, dee*
aeroplane	**Flugzeug, das**	*floogtsoyg, dass*
again	**wieder**	*veeder*
ago	**vor**	*for*
AIDS	**AIDS**	*aids*
airmail	**Luftpost, die**	*luftposst, dee*
airport	**Flughafen, der**	*flooghaafen, der*
alarm	**Wecker, der**	*vecker, der*
all	**all/e**	*al/alluh*
all right	**Ordnung (in)**	*ordnung (in)*
allergy	**Allergie, die**	*allergee, dee*
ambulance	**Krankenwagen, der**	*krankenvahgen, der*
America	**Amerika**	*amereekah*
American	**Amerikaner/in**	*amehreekahner/in*
and	**und**	*unt*

anniversary	**Jahrestag, der**	*yahruhstaag, der*

Germany celebrates the Anniversary of German Unity each October 3. The holiday has been a national one since 1990.

another	**noch eine/n/s**	*nokh eyenuh/en/s*
to answer	**antworten**	*antvorten*
any	**irgendein/e**	*ihrgenteyn/uh*
apartment	**Apartment, das**	*apartment, dass*
appointment	**Verabredung, die**	*fehrappraydung, dee*
April	**April**	*appreel*
area	**Region, die**	*raygeeohn, dee*
area code	**Regionalkennzahl, die**	*raygeeohnkenntsahl, dee*
around	**rund um; zirka**	*runt um; tseerka*
to arrange	**einrichten**	*eyenrikhten*
arrival	**Ankunft, die**	*ankunft, dee*
art	**Kunst, die**	*kunst, dee*
to ask	**fragen**	*frahgen*
aspirin	**Aspirin, das**	*aspireen, dass*
at (time)	**am/bei/um**	*am/bye/um*
August	**August**	*owgoost*
Australia	**Australien**	*owstrahleeun*
Australian	**Australier/in**	*owstrahleeuh/in*
available	**verfügbar**	*ferfuegbar*
away	**weg**	*veck*

B

baby	**Baby, das**	*baby, dass*
back (body)	**Rücken, der**	*rueken, der*

back (place)	**hinten**	*hinten*
bad	**schlecht**	*schlekht*
baggage	**Gepäck, das**	*guhpeck, dass*
bar (pub)	**Bar, die**	*bar, dee*
bath	**Bad, das**	*baad, dass*
bathing cap	**Badehaube, die**	*baaduhhowbuh, dee*
to be	**sein**	*zighn*
beach	**Strand, der**	*strant, der*
because	**da**	*dah*
because of	**wegen**	*vehgen*
best	**Beste, der/die/das**	*bestuh, der/dee/dass*
better	**besser**	*bessuh*
between	**zwischen**	*tsvischen*
bicycle	**Fahrrad, das**	*fahrraad, dass*
big	**groß**	*grohss*
bill	**Rechnung, die**	*rechnung, dee*
bit (a)	**Bisschen, ein**	*bisshun, eyn*
boarding card	**Bordkarte, die**	*bortkartuh, dee*
book	**Buch, das**	*boukh, dass*
to book	**buchen**	*boukhen*
booking	**Buchung, die**	*boukhung, dee*
box office	**Kartenverkauf, der**	*kartenferkowf, der*
boy	**Junge, der**	*yunguh, der*
brother	**Bruder, der**	*brooduh, der*
bureau de change	**Wechselbüro, das**	*vechzellbyuroh, dass*
to burn	**brennen**	*brennen*
bus	**Bus, der**	*buss, der*
business	**Geschäft, das**	*guhschaeft, dass*
business class	**Businessclass, die**	*businessclass, dee*
but	**aber**	*arbuh*
to buy	**kaufen**	*cowfen*
by (air, car, etc)	**mit (dem Flugzeug, dem Auto, etc.)**	*mit (daym floogtsoyg, daym owtoe, etc.)*
by (beside)	**neben**	*nehben*
by (via)	**per**	*per*

C

café **Café, das** *caffay, dass*
Hawelka is one of Vienna's typical old-time coffee houses – a must, also for the house speciality **Buchteln** (little cakes).

calculator	**Rechenmaschine, die**	*reschenmascheenuh, dee*
to call	**rufen**	*roofen*
camera	**Kamera, die**	*kamuhra, dee*
can (to be able)	**können**	*kernen*
to cancel	**stornieren**	*schtorneeren*
car	**Auto, das/Wagen, der**	*owtoh, dass/vahgen, der*

carnival	**Fasching, der**	_fassching, der_

Cities across the German-speaking region widely celebrate Carnival (**Fasching** or **Fasnacht**) with balls and colourful parades.

carton (cigarettes)	**Karton, der**	_karton, der_
cash	**Bargeld, das**	_bargelt, dass_
cashpoint	**Kasse, die**	_kassuh, dee_
casino	**Casino, das**	_caseeno, das_
castle	**Burg, die/Schloss, das**	_borg, dee/schloss, dass_
cathedral	**Kathedrale, die**	_kataydrahluh, dee_
cd	**CD, die**	_sayday, dee_
centre	**Zentrum, das**	_tsentroom, dass_
to change	**wechseln**	_vechseln_
charge	**Gebühr, die**	_guhbuehr, dee_
to charge	**berechnen**	_buhreshnen_
cheap	**billig**	_billig_
to check in (hotel, airport)	**einchecken**	_eyenshecken_
cheque	**Scheck, der**	_scheck, der_
child	**Kind, das**	_kint, dass_
to choose	**wählen**	_vaylen_
cigar	**Zigarre, die**	_tsigarruh, dee_
cigarette	**Zigarette, die**	_tsigarrettuh, dee_
cinema	**Kino, das**	_keenoh, dass_
city	**Stadt, die**	_schtadt, dee_
to close	**schließen**	_schleessen_
close by	**nahe/nahe bei**	_nahhuh/nahhuh bye_
closed	**geschlossen**	_guhschlossen_
clothes	**Kleidung, die**	_klydung, dee_
club	**Club, der**	_club, der_
coast	**Küste, die**	_kueste, dee_
coffee house	**Kaffeehaus, das**	_kaffayhowss, dass_
cold	**kalt**	_kalt_
colour	**Farbe, die**	_farbuh, dee_
to complain	**sich beschweren**	_zikh buhschvehren_
complaint	**Beschwerde, die**	_buhschvehrduh, dee_
to confirm	**bestätigen**	_buhschtaytigen_
confirmation	**Bestätigung, die**	_buhschtaytigung, dee_
congratulations!	**Herzlichen Glückwunsch!**	_herzlikhen glueckvunsch!_
consulate	**Konsulat, das**	_konzoolaat, dass_
to contact	**kontaktieren**	_kontakteerren_
contagious	**ansteckend**	_anschteckent_
cool	**kühl**	_kewhl_
cost	**Kosten, die**	_kosten, dee_
to cost	**kosten**	_kosten_
cot	**Kinderbett, das**	_kinderbett, dass_
country	**Land, das**	_lant, dass_
countryside	**Landschaft, die**	_lantschaft, dee_
cream	**Creme, die/ Sahne, die**	_crem, dee/zahnuh, dee_
credit card	**Kreditkarte, die**	_kraydeetkartuh, dee_

crime	**Verbrechen, das**	*ferbreschen, dass*
currency	**Währung, die**	*vaehrung, dee*
customer	**Kunde, der**	*kunduh, der*
customs	**Zoll, der**	*tsohl, der*
cut	**Schnitt, der**	*schnitt, der*
to cut	**schneiden**	*schnyden*
cycling	**Radsport, der**	*raadschport, der*

D

damage	**Schaden, der**	*schaaden, der*
date (calendar)	**Datum, das**	*daatomb, dass*
daughter	**Tochter, die**	*tokhtuh, dee*
day	**Tag, der**	*taag, der*
December	**Dezember**	*detsember*
to dehydrate	**dehydrieren**	*dayheedreeren*
delay	**Verspätung, die**	*ferspaetung, dee*
to dial	**wählen**	*vaylen*
difficult	**schwierig**	*schveerig*
dining room	**Speisesaal, der**	*schpighsuhzaal, der*
directions	**Anleitung, die**	*anlyteung, dee*
dirty	**schmutzig**	*schmutzig*
disabled	**behindert**	*buhhindert*
disco	**Disco, die**	*disko, dee*
discount	**Rabatt, der**	*rabaat, der*
disinfectant	**Desinfektions-mittel, das**	*desinfektiohnsmittel, dass*
district	**Viertel, das**	*feartel, dass*
to disturb	**stören**	*schtoeren*
doctor	**Arzt, der/Ärztin, die**	*arzt, der/erztin, dee*
double	**doppelt**	*doppelt*
down	**hinunter/unten**	*hinunter/unten*
to drive	**fahren**	*fahrren*
driver	**Fahrer, der/ Fahrerin, die**	*fahrruh, der/ fahrruhrin, dee*
driving licence	**Führerschein, der**	*fuehrerschine, der*
drug	**Droge, die**	*drohguh, dee*
to dry clean	**trocken reinigen**	*trocken rhinenigun*
dry-cleaner's	**chemische Reinigung, die**	*kaymische rhinei- gung, dee*
during	**während**	*vehrrent*
duty (tax)	**Gebühr, die/ Steuer, die**	*guhbuehr, dee/ schtoyuh, dee*

E

early	**früh**	*frueh*
e-mail	**E-mail, die**	*e-mail, dee*
embassy	**Botschaft, die**	*bohtschaft, dee*
emergency	**Notfall, der**	*nohtfal, der*
England	**England**	*ennglant*
English	**Englisch**	*ennglissh*
enough	**genug**	*guhnoog*
entrance	**Eingang, der**	*eyengang, der*
error	**Fehler, der**	*fehler, der*
exactly	**genau**	*guhnow*
exchange rate	**Wechselkurs, der**	*vekhselcourse, der*

exhibition	**Ausstellung, die**	_owssschtellung, dee_
exit	**Ausgang, der**	_owssgang, der_
express (delivery)	**Expresszustellung, die**	_expresstsuschtellung, dee_
express (train)	**Eilzug, der**	_eyltsoog, der_

F

facilities	**Einrichtungen, die**	_eynrikhtungen, dee_
far	**weit**	_vight_
father	**Vater, der**	_fahtuh, der_
favourite	**Lieblings-**	_leeblings-_
February	**Februar**	_fehbruar_

| festivals | **Festspiele, die** | _festspeeluh, dee_ |

The **Salzburger** and **Bregenzer Festspiele** are Austria's top summer events, attracting theatre and opera fans to performances in Salzburg's city centre and the stage on Lake Constance respectively.

filling (station)	**Tankstelle, die**	_tankschtelluh, dee_
film (camera)	**Film, der**	_feelm, der_
film (cinema)	**Kinofilm, der**	_keenofeelm, der_
fire	**Feuer, das**	_foyer, dass_
first aid	**Erste Hilfe**	_erstuh hillfuh_
fitting room	**Umkleidekabine, die**	_umklyduhkahbeenuh, dee_
flight	**Flug, der**	_floog, der_
flu	**Grippe, die**	_grippuh, dee_
food poisoning	**Lebensmittel-vergiftung, die**	_lebensmittel-fergiftung, dee_
football	**Fußball, der**	_fussbal, der_
for	**für**	_fuer_
form (document)	**Formular, das**	_formoolah, dass_
free	**frei**	_fry_
free (money)	**gratis**	_grahteece_
friend	**Freund, der/ Freundin, die**	_froynt, der/ froyntin, dee_
from	**von**	_fon_

G

gallery	**Gallerie, die**	_galleree, dee_
garage (repair)	**Reparaturwerkstatt, die**	_reparahaa-torverkschtatt, dee_
gas	**Gas, das**	_gaas, das_
gents	**Herrentoilette, die**	_herrentwighlettuh, dee_
German	**Deutsch**	_doitsch_

| Germany | **Deutschland** | _doitschlant_ |

February sees Berlin's largest cultural event, the International Film Festival Berlinale

girl	**Mädchen, das**	_maidshen, das_
glasses (spectacles)	**Brille, die**	_brilluh, dee_
golf	**Golf**	_gohlf_

| golf course | **Golfplatz, der** | _gohlfplatz, der_ |

Golf courses have mushroomed in Austria over the past few years, often located in wonderful alpine panorama.

good	**gut**	_goot_
group	**Gruppe, die**	_gruppuh, dee_
guarantee	**Garantie, die**	_guarantee, dee_
guide	**Reiseführer, der**	_righzuhfuehruh, der_

H

hair	**Haar, das**	_haar, dass_
hairdresser's	**Frisör, der**	_freesoer, der_
half	**halb**	_halp_
heat	**Hitze, die**	_hitzuh, dee_
help!	**Hilfe!**	_hillfuh!_
here	**hier**	_heeuh_
high	**hoch, hohe/r/s**	_hokh, hohhuh/r/s_
holiday (work-free day)	**Feiertag, der**	_foyertaag, der_
holidays	**Urlaub, der**	_uhrlowp, der_
homosexual	**homosexuell**	_hohmozekszooell_
hospital	**Krankenhaus, das**	_krankenhowss, dass_
hot	**heiß**	_hice_
how?	**wie?**	_vee?_
how big?	**wie groß?**	_vee grohss?_
how far?	**wie weit?**	_vee vight?_
how long?	**wie lange?**	_vee languh?_
how much?	**wieviel?**	_veefeel?_
hurry up!	**beeilen Sie sich!**	_buheyelen zee zikh!_
husband	**Ehemann, der/ Gatte, der**	_ehuhman, der/gattuh, der_

I

identity card	**Identitätskarte, die**	_eedentitaetskahrtuh, dee_
ill	**krank**	_krank_
immediately	**sofort**	_zofort_
important	**wichtig**	_vishtig_
in	**in**	_in_
information	**Information, die**	_informatiohn, dee_
inside	**drinnen/innen**	_drinnen/innen_
insurance	**Versicherung, die**	_fersisherung, dee_
interesting	**interessant**	_interesssant_
international	**international**	_internattionsional_
Ireland	**Irland**	_ihrlant_
Irish	**Irisch**	_ihrish_
island	**Insel, die**	_inzel, dee_
itinerary	**Reiseroute, die**	_righzuhrootuh, dee_

J

January	**Januar**	_yanuar_
jet ski	**Jet-Ski, der**	_jet-ski, der_
journey	**Reise, die**	_righzuh, dee_
July	**Juli**	_yuhlee_
junction	**Abzweigung, die**	_abtsvighgung, dee_

| June | **Juni** | *yuhnee* |
| just (only) | **nur** | *noor* |

K

key	**Schlüssel, der**	*schluessel, der*
keyring	**Schlüsselring, der**	*schluesselring, der*
keyboard	**Tastatur, die**	*tasttator, dee*
kid	**Kind, das**	*kint, dass*
kind	**nett**	*nett*
kind (person)	**sympathisch**	*zympaatish*
kind (sort)	**Sorte, die**	*zortuh, dee*
kiosk	**Kiosk, der**	*kiosk, der*
kiss	**Kuss, der**	*kuss, der*

L

label	**Marke, die**	*markuh, dee*
ladies (toilets)	**Damen(toilette), die**	*dahmen(twighlettuh), dee*
lady	**Dame, die**	*dahmuh, dee*
lake	**See, die**	*zay, dee*
language	**Sprache, die**	*schpraachhuh, dee*
last	**letzte/r/s**	*letztuh/r/s*
late (delayed)	**verspätet**	*ferspaetet*
late (time)	**spät**	*spaet*
launderette	**Waschsalon, der**	*vashzallohn, der*
lawyer	**abreisen**	*apprighzen*
less	**weniger**	*vehniguh*

| library | **Brief, der** | *brief, der* |

After reunification, three institutions in Leipzig, Frankfurt and Berlin combined to form the German National Library.

---

life jacket	**Rettungsweste, die**	*rettungsvestuh, dee*
lifeguard	**Rettungs-schwimmer, der**	*rettungs-schwimmer, der*
lift	**Fahrstuhl, der**	*fahrschtuhl, der*
like	**gernhaben/mögen**	*gernhabhen/mergen*
little	**etwas**	*etvass*
local	**lokal**	*lohkahl*
to lose	**verlieren**	*ferleeren*
lost property	**verlorene Gegenstände**	*ferlorennuh gehgen-schtenduh*
luggage	**Reisegepäck, das**	*righzuhguhpeck, dass*

M

madam	**gnädige Frau**	*gnaydiguh frau*
mail	**Post, die**	*posst, dee*
main	**Haupt-**	*howpt-*
man	**Mann, der**	*man, der*
manager	**Manager, der**	*manager, der*
many	**viele**	*feeluh*
map (city)	**Stadtplan, der**	*schtatplan, der*
map (road)	**Autokarte, die**	*owtoekartuh, dee*
March	**März**	*mehrz*

market   **Markt, der**   *markt, der*
Across the region there are marvellous Christmas
markets. Many shoppers keep warm with **Glühwein**
(hot mulled wine).

married	**verheiratet**	*ferhighraatet*
May	**Mai**	*my*
maybe	**vielleicht**	*feellighscht*
mechanic	**Mechaniker, der**	*mecaanikuh, der*
meeting	**Meeting, das**	*meeting, das*
message	**Nachricht, die**	*nakhrischt, dee*
midday	**Mittag, der**	*mittaag, der*
midnight	**Mitternacht, die**	*mitternahkt, dee*
minimum	**Mindest-**	*mindest-*
minute	**Minute, die**	*meenootuh, dee*
missing	**vermisst**	*fermisst*
mobile phone	**Handy, das/**	*hendy, dass/mohbeal-*
	Mobiltelefon, das	*telefohn dass*
moment	**Moment, der**	*mohment, der*
money	**Geld, das**	*gelt, das*
more	**mehr**	*mehr*
mosquito	**Mücke, die**	*mueckuh, dee*
most	**meist/am meisten**	*mighst/am mighsten*
mother	**Mutter, die**	*muttuh, dee*
much	**viel**	*fiel*

museum   **Museum, das**   *moozayum, dass*
The **Museumsquartier**, with its cafés and restaurants,
is one of Vienna's coolest hangouts, home to the Leopold
Museum and the MUMOK (Museum of Modern Art).

musical	**Musical, das**	*moozikaal, das*
must	**müssen**	*muessen*
my	**mein/meine**	*mine/mynuh*

N

name	**Name, der**	*nahmuh, der*
nationality	**Nationalität, die**	*natsionalitayte, dee*
near	**nahe/nahe bei**	*nahhuh/nahhuh bye*
necessary	**notwendig**	*nohtvendig*
never	**niemals**	*neemals*
new	**neu**	*noy*
news	**Nachrichten, die**	*nakhrikhten, dee*
newspaper	**Tageszeitung, die**	*taaguhstsighttung, dee*
next	**nächste/r/s**	*nekhschtuh/ter/tes*
next to	**neben**	*nehben*
nice	**nett**	*nett*
nice (people)	**sympathisch**	*zympaatish*
night	**Nacht, die**	*nahkt, dee*
nightclub	**Nachtklub, der**	*nakhtklub, der*
north	**Norden, der**	*norden, der*
note (message)	**Nachricht, die**	*nakhrischt, dee*
note (money)	**Geldschein, der**	*geltschine, der*
nothing	**nichts**	*nikhts*

November	**November**	*nofember*
now	**jetzt**	*yetzt*
nowhere	**nirgendwo**	*nihrgentvo*
nudist beach	**Nudistenstrand, der**	*noodistenschtrant, der*
number (figure)	**Zahl, die**	*tsaahl, dee*
number (of items)	**Anzahl, die**	*antsaahl, dee*

O

object	**Gegenstand, der**	*gehgenschtant, der*
October	**Oktober**	*oktohbuh*
off (switched)	**ausgeschaltet**	*owssguhschalltet*
office	**Büro, das**	*byuroh, dass*
ok	**okay**	*okay*
on	**an/auf**	*an/owf*
once	**einmal**	*eyenmal*
only	**nur**	*noor*
open	**geöffnet**	*guherfnet*
to open	**öffnen**	*erfnen*
operator	**Telefonist/in, der/die**	*telefohnist/in, der/dee*
opposite (place)	**gegenüber**	*gehgenewber*
optician's	**Optiker, der**	*optikuh, der*
or	**oder**	*ohduh*
other	**andere/r/s**	*anderah/r/s*
out of order	**außer Betrieb**	*owssuh betreeb*
outdoor	**Freien (im)**	*fryen (im)*
outside	**draußen/außen**	*drowssen/owssen*
overnight	**über Nacht**	*ewber nahkt*
owner	**Besitzer/in, der/die**	*buhzitser/in, der/dee*
oxygen	**Sauerstoff, der**	*zowuhschtoff, der*

P

painkiller	**Schmerzmittel, das**	*schmerzmittel, dass*
pair	**Paar, das**	*paar, dass*
parents	**Eltern, die**	*eltern, dee*
park	**Park, der**	*park, der*
parking	**Parkplatz, der**	*parkplatz, der*
party	**Party, die**	*party, dee*
passport	**Reisepass, der**	*righzuhpass, der*
people	**Leute, die**	*loytuh, dee*
perhaps	**vielleicht**	*feellighscht*
person	**Person, die**	*perzohn, dee*
petrol	**Benzin, das**	*bentseen, dass*
photo	**Foto, das**	*fohtoh, dass*
phrase book	**Sprachführer, der**	*schprachfuehruh, der*
place	**Ort, der/Platz, der**	*ort, der/platz, der*
platform	**Bahnsteig, der**	*bahnschtighg, der*
police	**Polizei, die**	*poleetsigh, dee*
port (sea)	**Hafen, der**	*haafen, der*
possible	**möglich**	*merglish*
post	**Post, die**	*posst, dee*
post office	**Postamt, das**	*posstamt, dass*
prescription	**ärztliche Rezept, das**	*erztlishuh retsept, dass*

price	**Preis, der**	*price, der*
private	**privat**	*preevaat*
probably	**wahrscheinlich**	*vahrschineleesh*
problem	**Problem, das**	*prohblehm, das*

| **pub** | **Kneipe, die** | *kniypuh, dee* |

For a cosy evening get-together, choose a traditional
Bierkneipe (pub) in Cologne's old city.

| public transport | **öffentliche Verkehr, der** | *erfentlishuh ferkehr, der* |

Q
quality	**Qualität, die**	*qvalitayt, dee*
quantity	**Menge, die**	*mengguh, dee*
quarter (district)	**Viertel, das**	*feartel, dass*
query	**Anfrage, die**	*anfraaguh, dee*
question	**Frage, die**	*fraaguh, dee*
queue	**Schlange, die**	*schlangguh, dee*
quick	**rasch/schnell**	*rasch/schnell*
quickly	**rasch/schnell**	*rasch/schnell*
quiet	**ruhig**	*roohig*
quite	**ziemlich**	*tseemlikh*
quiz	**Quiz, das**	*qviz, dass*

R
radio	**Radio, das**	*raadio, das*
railway	**(Eisen-)Bahn, die**	*(eyesen-)bahn, dee*
rain	**Regen, der**	*rehgen, der*
rape	**Vergewaltigung, die**	*ferguhvaltigung, dee*
razor blade	**Rasierklinge, die**	*razeerklinguh, dee*
ready	**fertig**	*fertig, dee*
real	**wirklich**	*virklish*
receipt	**Beleg, der**	*belayg, der*
receipt (shopping)	**Kassenzettel, der**	*kassentsettel, der*
reception	**Rezeption, die**	*retseptiohn, dee*
receptionist	**Rezeptionist/in, der/die**	*retseptiohnist/in, der/dee*
recipe	**Rezept, das**	*retsept, dass*
reduction	**Ermäßigung, die**	*ermaysigung, dee*
refund	**Rückvergütung, die**	*rueckferguetung, dee*
regional	**regional**	*raygeeohnnal*
to relax	**entspannen**	*entschpannen*
rent	**Miete, die**	*meetuh, dee*
reservation	**Reservierung, die**	*reserveerung, dee*
retired	**pensioniert**	*punsiohneeert*
rich	**anrufen**	*anroofen*
road	**Straße, die**	*schtraassuh, dee*
room	**Zimmer, das**	*tsimmuh, dass*

| **route** | **Route, die** | *rootuh, dee* |

Bike routes trace the Rhine and fan into the countryside.
Add a short river cruise for another perspective.

| rude | **unhöflich** | *unhoeflikh* |

| ruins | **Ruinen, die** | _rooeeenen, dee_ |
| to run | **rennen** | _rennen_ |

S

safe	**sicher**	_zishher_
sauna	**Sauna, die**	_zowna, dee_
Scotland	**Schottland**	_schottlant_
Scottish	**Schottisch**	_schotttish_
sea	**Meer, das**	_mehr, dass_
seat	**Sitz, der**	_zitz, der_
seat belt	**Sicherheitsgurt, der**	_zisherheightsgort, der_
sedative	**Beruhigungs-mittel, das**	_buhroohigungsmittel, dass_
see you later!	**Bis später!**	_biss schpaytuh!_
self-service	**Selbstbedienung, die**	_zelbstbuhdeenung, dee_
sensible	**vernünftig**	_fernuenftig_
sensitive	**empfindlich**	_empfintlikh_
September	**September**	_zeptembuh_
to serve	**bedienen**	_buhdeenen_
service	**Service, der**	_serveecesuh, der_
shop	**Laden, der**	_laaden, der_
shopping	**Einkaufen, das**	_eyncowfen, dass_
shopping centre	**Einkaufszentrum, das**	_eyncowfstsentroom, dass_
short	**kurz**	_korz_
to show	**zeigen**	_tsighgen_
shut	**geschlossen**	_guhschlossen_
sign	**Zeichen, das**	_tsighchen, dass_
signature	**Unterschrift, die**	_unterschrift, dee_
since	**seit**	_zight_
sir	**Herr**	_herr_
sister	**Schwester, die**	_schvesstuh, dee_

| **ski** | **Ski, der** | _schee, der_ |

There's a good chance you'll meet Roger Moore in St Moritz, Switzerland's poshest skiing resort.

sleeping pill	**Schlaftablette, die**	_schlaaftablettuh, dee_
slow	**langsam**	_langzaam_
small	**klein**	_kline_
soft	**weich**	_veikh_
some	**einige**	_eyniguh_
something	**etwas/irgendetwas**	_etwass/ihrgentetvass_
son	**Sohn, der**	_zohn, der_
soon	**bald**	_balt_
south	**Süden, der**	_zueden, der_
South Africa	**Südafrika**	_zuedafreeka_
South African	**Südafrikaner/in**	_zuedafreekaanuh/in_
speed	**Geschwindigkeit, die**	_guhschvindigkite, dee_
sport	**Sport, der**	_schport, der_
stadium	**Stadium, das**	_schtaadium, dass_
staff	**Personal, das**	_perzonaal, das_
stamp	**(Brief-)Marke, die**	_(brief-)markuh, dee_

station	**Station, die**	*schtatiohn, dee*
sterling pound	**Pfund Sterling**	*pfunt schterling*
still	**noch**	*nokh*
stomach ulcer	**Magengeschwür, das**	*maagenguhschvurrh, das*
straight	**gerade**	*guhraaduh*

| **street** | **Straße, die** | *schtraassuh, dee* |

Zürich's **Bahnhofstrasse** is the country's number one shopping venue, not just for chocolate and watches but also for fashion and antiques.

stress	**Stress, der**	*schtress, der*
suddenly	**plötzlich**	*plertzlish*
suitcase	**Koffer, der**	*koffuh, der*
sun	**Sonne, die**	*zonnuh, dee*
sunglasses	**Sonnenbrille, die**	*zonnenbrilluh, dee*
surname	**Nachname, der**	*nakhnahmuh, der*
swimming pool	**Schwimmbad, das**	*schvimmbaad, dass*
switched on	**eingeschaltet**	*eynguhschalltet*
symptom	**Symptom, das**	*zumptohm, dass*

T

table	**Tisch, der**	*tisch, der*
to take	**nehmen**	*nehmen*
tall	**groß**	*grohss*
tampons	**Tampons, die**	*tampohns, dee*
tax	**Steuer, die**	*schtoyuh, dee*
tax free	**steuerfrei**	*schtoyuhfry*
taxi	**Taxi, das**	*taxee, das*
taxi rank	**Taxistand, der**	*taxeeschtant, der*
telephone	**Telefon, das**	*telefohn, dass*
telephone box	**Telefonzelle, die**	*telefohnschtelluh, dee*
television	**Fernsehen, das**	*fernzehen, dass*
tennis	**Tennis**	*tenneece*
tennis court	**Tennisplatz, der**	*tenneeceplatz, der*
terrace	**Terrasse, die**	*terrassuh, dee*
to text	**eine SMS senden**	*eyenuh ess-m-ess zenden*
that	**das**	*dass*
theft	**Diebstahl, der**	*deebschtaal, der*
then	**dann**	*dan*
there	**dort/da**	*dort/dah*
thing	**Ding, das**	*ding, dass*

| **to think** | **denken** | *denken* |

Germany – home to many famous writers and philosophers – is often called the Nation of Poets and Thinkers.

thirsty	**denken**	*dorstig*
this	**dies**	*deece*
through	**durch**	*dorsch*
ticket (bus)	**Fahrkarte, die**	*fahrkartuh, dee*
ticket (cinema)	**Eintrittskarte, die**	*eyentrittskartuh, dee*
ticket (parking)	**Strafzettel, der**	*straaftsettel, der*

English	German	Pronunciation
ticket office	Kartenschalter, der	_kartenschaltuh, der_
time	Zeit, die	_tsight, dee_
time (clock)	Uhrzeit, die	_uhrtsight, dee_
timetable	Fahrplan, der	_fahrplan, der_
tip (money)	Trinkgeld, das	_trinkgelt, dass_
tired	müde	_mewduh_
to	nach/zu	_nakh/tsu_
to (the left/right/ upstairs)	nach (links/ rechts/oben)	_nakh (links/rekhts/ohben)_
tobacco	Tabak, der	_tabak, der_
today	heute	_hoytuh_
toilet	Toilette, die	_twighlettuh, dee_
toiletries	Toilettenartikel, die	_twighlettenarteekel, dee_
toll	Maut, die	_mowt, dee_
tomorrow	morgen	_morgen_
tonight	heute Abend/ Nacht	_hoytuh ahbent/nakht_
too	auch	_owkch_
tourist office	Fremdenver- kehrsbüro, das	_fremdenferkehrs- byuroh dass_
town	Stadt, die	_schtadt, dee_
town hall	Rathaus, das	_raat-howss, dass_
train	Zug, der	_tsoog, der_
tram	Straßenbahn, die	_straassenbaahn, dee_
to translate	übersetzen	_ewberzetsen_
to travel	reisen	_righzuhn_
travel agency	Reiseagentur, die	_righzuhahgentor, dee_
true (fact)	wahr	_vahr_
true (right)	richtig	_rikhtig_
typical	typisch	_toopisch_

U

ugly	hässlich	_hesslikh_
ulcer	Geschwür, das	_guhschvurrh, das_
umbrella	Regenschirm, der	_rehgenscheerm, der_
uncomfortable	unbequem	_unbuhqvehm_
unconscious	bewusstlos	_buhvusstlohss_
under	unter	_unter_
underground (tube)	U-Bahn, die	_oo-bahn, dee_
to understand	verstehen	_ferstehen_
underwear	Unterwäsche, die	_untervaeschhuh, dee_
unemployed	arbeitslos	_arbiteslohss_
unpleasant	unangenehm	_unanguhnehm_
up	hinauf	_hinowf_
upstairs	oben	_ohben_
urgent	dringend	_dringent_
to use	benutzen	_buhnutzen_
useful	nützlich	_nuetzlikh_
usually	normalerweise	_normaaluhvysuh_

V

vacant	frei	_fry_
vacation	Ferien, die	_fehrieen, dee_
vaccination	Impfung, die	_impfung, dee_

valid	gültig	gueltig
valuables	Wertsachen, die	vertzakhen, dee
value	Wert, der	vert, der
VAT	Mehrwertsteuer, die	mehrvertstoyuh, dee
vegetarian	Vegetarier/in, der/die	vegetaryer/in, der/dee
vehicle	Fahrzeug, das	fahrtsoyg, dass
very	sehr	zehr
visa	Visum, das	veezum, dass
visit	Besuch, der	buhzukh, der
to visit	besuchen	buhzukhen
vitamin	Vitamin, das	vitameen, dass
to vomit	sich übergeben	zikh ewbuhgehben

W

waiter/waitress	kellner, der /kellnerin, die	kellner, der /Kellnerin, die

Tip five per cent of the invoiced amount, unless dining at a ritzier restaurant, where ten per cent is more gracious.

waiting room	Wartezimmer, das	wartuhtsimmuh, dass
Wales	Wales	vales
to walk	gehen	gehhen
wallet	Geldtasche, die	gelttaschhuh, dee
to want	wollen	vollen
to wash	waschen	vaschen
watch	anschauen/ beobachten	anschowen/ buhohbakhten
water	Wasser, das	vasser, dass
water sports	Wassersport, der	vasserschport, der
way (manner)	Art und Weise, die	art unt viseuh, dee
way (route)	Weg, der	veck, der
way in	Eingang, der	eyengang, der
way out	Ausgang, der	owssgang, der
weather	Wetter, das	vettuh, dass
web	Web, das	web, das
website	Webseite, die	webzightuh, dee
week	Woche, die	vochhuh, dee
weekday	Wochentag, der	vochentaag, der
weekend	Wochenende, das	vochhenendduh, dass
welcome	willkommen	villkommen
well	gut	goot
Welsh	Walisisch	valeesish
west	Westen, der	vesten, der
what?	was?	vass?
wheelchair	Rollstuhl, der	rohlschtool, der
when?	wann?	vann?
where?	wo?	vo?
which?	welche/r/s?	velchuh/r/s?
while	während	vehrrent
who?	wer?	vehr?
why?	warum?/weshalb?	varrum?/vesshalp?
wife	Ehefrau, die/ Gattin, die	ehhuhfrau, dee/ gattin, dee
to win	gewinnen	guhvinnen

with	**mit**	*mit*
without	**ohne**	*ohnnuh*
woman	**Frau, die**	*frau, dee*

| **wonderful** | **wunderbar** | *vunderbah* |

Wonderful German wines grow on the hills along the Rhine, from Lake Constance to Bonn.

word	**Wort, das**	*vort, dass*
work	**Arbeit, die**	*ahrbite, dee*
to work (machine)	**funktionieren**	*funkteeohnneerren*
to work (person)	**arbeiten**	*ahrbiteten*
world	**Welt, die**	*velt, dee*
worried	**besorgt**	*buhzorgt*
worse	**schlechter**	*schleshtuh*
to write	**schreiben**	*schrighben*
wrong (mistaken)	**falsch**	*falsch*

X

xenophobe	**Fremdenhasser/ in, der/die**	*fremdenhasser/in, der/dee*
xenophobia	**Fremdenfeind- lichkeit, die**	*fremdenfighntlishkite, dee*
x-ray	**Röntgenauf-nahme, die**	*rerntgenowfnahmuh, dee*
to x-ray	**röntgen**	*rerntgen*
x-rays	**Röntgenstrahlen, die**	*rerntgenschtraahlen, dee*

Y

yacht	**Yacht, die**	*yacht, dee*
year	**Jahr, das**	*yahr, dass*
yearly	**jährlich**	*yerlich*
yellow pages	**Gelben Seiten, die**	*gelben zighten, dee*
yes	**ja**	*yaah*
yesterday	**gestern**	*gestern*
yet	**schon**	*schohn*
you (formal)	**Sie**	*zee*
you (informal)	**du**	*du*
young	**jung**	*yung*
your (formal)	**Ihr/e**	*ihr/era*
your (informal)	**dein/deine**	*dine/dynuh*
youth hostel	**Jugendherberge, die**	*yugentherberguh, dee*

Z

zebra crossing	**Zebrastreifen, der**	*tsaybraschtryfen, der*
zero	**null**	*null*
zip	**Reisverschluss, der**	*riceferschluss, der*
zone	**Zone, die**	*tsohnuh, dee*
zoo	**Tierpark, der/Zoo, der**	*teerpark, der/tsoh, der*

A

aber	_arbuh_	but
abreisen	_apprighzen_	to leave
Abzweigung, die	_abtsvighgung, dee_	junction
AIDS	_aids_	AIDS
all/e	_al/alluh_	all
Allergie, die	_allergee, dee_	allergy
am	_am_	at
Amerika	_amereekah_	America
Amerikaner/in	_amehreekahner/in_	American
an	_an_	on
andere/r/s	_anderuh/r/s_	other
Anfrage, die	_anfraaguh, dee_	query
anhalten	_anhalten_	to stop
Ankunft, die	_ankunft, dee_	arrival
Anleitung, die	_anlyteung, dee_	directions
anrufen	_anroofen_	to ring/to phone
anschauen	_anschowen_	to watch
ansteckend	_anschteckent_	contagious
antworten	_antvorten_	to answer
Anwalt, der	_anvalt, der_	lawyer
Anzahl, die	_antsaahl, dee_	number
Apartment, das	_apartment, dass_	apartment
April	_appreel_	April
Arbeit, die	_ahrbite, dee_	work
arbeiten	_ahrbiteten_	to work (person)
arbeitslos	_arbiteslohss_	unemployed

Armbanduhr, die   _ahrmbantuhr, dee_   watch
Handmade precision watches are Switzerland's best-
known handicraft. They take a month to produce –
and a big purse to buy!

Art und Weise, die	_art und viseuh, dee_	way (manner)
Arzt, der/Ärztin, die	_arzt, der/erztin, dee_	doctor
ärztliche Rezept, das	_erztlishuh retsept, dass_	prescription
Aspirin, das	_aspireen, dass_	aspirin
auch	_owkch_	too
auf	_owf_	on
August	_owgoost_	August
Ausgang, der	_owssgang, der_	way out
ausgeschaltet	_owssguhschalltet_	off (switched)
ausrauben	_owssrowben_	to rob
außen	_owssen_	outside
außer Betrieb	_owssuh betreeb_	out of order
Ausstellung, die	_owssschtellung, dee_	exhibition
Australien	_owstrahleeun_	Australia
Australier/in	_owstrahleeuh/in_	Australian
Auto, das	_owtoh, dass_	car
Autokarte, die	_owtoekartuh, dee_	map (road)

B

German	Pronunciation	English
Baby, das	*baby, dass*	baby
Bad, das	*baad, dass*	bath
Badehaube, die	*baaduhhowbuh, dee*	bathing cap
Bahn, die	*bahn, dee*	railway
Bahnsteig, der	*bahnschtighg, der*	platform
bald	*balt*	soon
Bar, die	*bar, dee*	bar (pub)
Bargeld, das	*bargelt, dass*	cash
bedienen	*buhdeenen*	to serve
Beeilen Sie sich!	*buheyelen zee zikh!*	hurry up!
beenden	*buhenden*	to finish
beginnen	*beginnen*	to start
behindert	*buhhindert*	disabled
bei	*bye*	at
bekommen	*buhkommen*	to get
Beleg, der	*belayg, der*	receipt
benötigen	*buhnertigen*	to need
benutzen	*buhnutzen*	to use
Benzin, das	*bentseen, dass*	petrol
beobachten	*buhohbakhten*	to watch; to observe
berechnen	*buhreshnen*	to charge
Beruhigungsmittel, das	*buhroohigungsmittel, dass*	sedative
Beschwerde, die	*buhschvehrduh, dee*	complaint
Besitzer/in, der/die	*buhzitser/in, der/dee*	owner
besorgt	*buhzorgt*	worried
besser	*bessuh*	better
bestätigen	*buhschtaytigen*	to confirm
Bestätigung, die	*buhschtaytigung, dee*	confirmation
Beste, der/die/das	*bestuh, der/dee/dass*	best
bestellen	*buhschtellen*	to order
Besuch, der	*buhzukh, der*	visit
besuchen	*buhzukhen*	to visit
bevorzugen	*buhfortsugen*	to prefer
bewusstlos	*buhvusstlohss*	unconscious
bezahlen	*buhtsaahlen*	to pay
Bibliothek, die	*bibliotehk, dee*	library
billig	*billig*	cheap
Bis später!	*biss schpaytuh*	see you later
Bisschen, ein	*eyn bisshun*	bit (a)
Bordkarte, die	*bortkartuh, dee*	boarding card
Botschaft, die	*bohtschaft, dee*	embassy
brennen	*brennen*	to burn
Brief, der	*brief, der*	letter
Briefmarke, die	*briefmarkuh, dee*	stamp
Brille, die	*brilluh, dee*	glasses (spectacles)
Bruder, der	*brooduh, der*	brother

Buch, das	***boukh, dass***	**book**

In 2006, the German Producer Bernd Eichinger filmed the famous book *Perfume*, written by Patrick Süskind.

buchen	*boukhen*	to book

buchstabieren	*bukhschtabeeren*	to spell
Buchung, die	*boukhung, dee*	booking
Burg, die	*borg, dee*	castle
Büro, das	*byuroh, dass*	office
Bus, der	*buss, der*	bus
Businessclass, die	*businessclass, dee*	business class

C

Café, das	*caffay, dass*	café
Casino, das	*caseeno, das*	casino
CD, die	*sayday, dee*	cd
chemische Reinigung, die	*kaymische rhineigung, dee*	dry-cleaner's
Club, der	*club, der*	club
Creme, die	*crem, dee*	cream

D

da	*dah*	there; because
Dame, die	*dahmuh, dee*	lady
Damentoilette, die	*dahmentwighlettuh, dee*	ladies (toilets)
dann	*dan*	then
das	*dass*	that
Datum, das	*daatomb, dass*	date (calendar)
dehydrieren	*dayheedreeren*	to dehydrate
dein/deine	*dine/dynuh*	your (informal)
denken	*denken*	to think
Desinfektionsmittel, das	*desinfektiohnsmittel, dass*	disinfectant

| **Deutsch** | *doitsch* | **German** |

German is just one of four official languages in Switzerland. The others are French, Italian and Romansh.

Deutschland	*doitschlant*	Germany
Dezember	*detsember*	December
Diebstahl, der	*deebschtaal, der*	theft
dies	*deece*	this
Ding, das	*ding, dass*	thing
Disco, die	*disko, dee*	disco
doppelt	*doppelt*	double
dort	*dort*	there
draußen	*drowssen*	outdoor; outside
dringend	*dringent*	urgent
drinnen	*drinnen*	inside
Droge, die	*drohguh, dee*	drug
du	*du*	you (informal)
durch	*dorsch*	through
durstig	*dorstig*	thirsty

E

Ehefrau, die	*ehhuhfrau, dee*	wife
Ehemann, der	*ehuhman, der*	husband
Eilzug, der	*eyltsoog, der*	express (train)
ein/eine	*eyn/eyenuh*	a(n)
einchecken	*eynshecken*	to check in (hotel,

Eingang, der	*eyengang, der*	way in
eingeschaltet	*eynguhschalltet*	(switched) on
einige	*eyniguh*	some

Einkaufen, das   *eyncowfen, dass*   shopping
Shopping at Vienna's **Naschmarkt**, the city's biggest
food market with a unique atmosphere, is a feast.
Visit the nearby flea market on Saturdays.

Einkaufszentrum, das	*eyncowfstsentroom, dass*	shopping centre
einmal	*eyenmal*	once
einrichten	*eyenrikhten*	to arrange
Einrichtungen, die	*eynrikhtungen, dee*	facilities
Eintrittskarte, die	*eyentrittskartuh, dee*	ticket (cinema)
Eisenbahn, die	*eyesenbahn, dee*	railway
Eltern, die	*eltern, dee*	parents
E-mail, die	*e-mail, dee*	e-mail
empfangen	*empfangen*	to receive
empfehlen	*empfehlen*	to recommend
empfindlich	*empfintlikh*	sensitive
England	*ennglant*	England
Englisch	*ennglissh*	English
entspannen	*entschpannen*	to relax
erbitten	*erbitten*	to request
erhalten	*erhalten*	to get
Ermäßigung, die	*ermaysigung, dee*	reduction
Erste Hilfe	*erstuh hillfuh*	first aid
essen	*essen*	to eat
etwas	*etvass*	something; little; a little
exportieren	*exporteeren*	to export
Expresszustellung, die	*expresstsuschtellung, dee*	express (delivery)

F

fahren	*fahrren*	to drive
Fahrer, der/ Fahrerin, die	*fahrruh, der/ fahrruhrin, dee*	driver
Fahrkarte, die	*fahrkartuh, dee*	ticket (bus)
Fahrplan, der	*fahrplan, der*	timetable
Fahrrad, das	*fahrraad, dass*	bicycle
Fahrstuhl, der	*fahrschtuhl, der*	lift
Fahrzeug, das	*fahrtsoyg, dass*	vehicle
falsch	*falsch*	wrong (mistaken)
Farbe, die	*farbuh, dee*	colour
Fasching, der	*fassching, der*	carnival
faxen	*faxen*	to fax
Februar	*fehbruar*	February
Fehler, der	*fehler, der*	error
Feiertag, der	*foyertaag, der*	holiday (work-free day)
Ferien, die	*fehrieen, dee*	vacation
Fernsehen, das	*fernzehen, dass*	television
fertig	*fertig, dee*	ready
Feuer, das	*foyer, dass*	fire

Festspiele, die   *festspeeluh, dee*   festivals
Opera fans from around the world assemble
annually at the Bayreuth Festival to honour
Richard Wagner's compositions.

Film, der	*feelm, der*	film; camera film
Flug, der	*floog, der*	flight
Flughafen, der	*flooghaafen, der*	airport
Flugzeug, das	*floogtsoyg, dass*	aeroplane
Formular, das	*formoolah, dass*	form (document)
Foto, das	*fohtoh, dass*	photo
Frage, die	*fraaguh, dee*	question
fragen	*frahgen*	to ask
Frau, die	*frau, dee*	woman
frei	*fry*	free; vacant
im Freien	*im fryen*	outdoor
Fremdenfeindlichkeit, die	*fremdenfighntlishkite, dee*	xenophobia
Fremdenhasser/in, der/die	*fremdenhasser/in, der/dee*	xenophobe
Fremdenverkehrsbüro, das	*fremdenferkehrsbyuroh, dass*	tourist office
Freund, der/ Freundin, die	*froynd, der/ froyndin, dee*	friend
Frisör, der	*freesoer, der*	hairdresser's
früh	*frueh*	early
Führerschein, der	*fuehrerschine, der*	driving licence
funktionieren	*funkteeohnneerren*	to work (machine)
für	*fuer*	for
Fußball, der	*fussbal, der*	football

G

Gallerie, die	*galleree, dee*	gallery
Garantie, die	*guarantee, dee*	guarantee
Gas, das	*gaas, das*	gas
Gatte, der	*gattuh, der*	husband
Gattin, die	*gattin, dee*	wife
geben	*gehben*	to give
Gebühr, die	*guhbuehr, dee*	charge; duty (tax)
Gegenstand, der	*gehgenschtant, der*	object
gegenüber	*gehgenewber*	opposite (place)
gehen	*gehhen*	to go; to walk
Gelben Seiten, die	*gelben zighten, dee*	yellow pages
Geldschein, der	*geltschine, der*	note (money)

Geld, das   *gelt, das*   money
Swiss Francs are still Switzerland's official currency,
though the euro is increasingly accepted in tourist
areas and big cities.

Geldtasche, die	*gelttaschhuh, dee*	wallet
genau	*guhnow*	exactly
genießen	*guhneesen*	to enjoy

German-English

German	Pronunciation	English
genug	*guhnoog*	enough
geöffnet	*guherfnet*	open
Gepäck, das	*guhpeck, dass*	baggage
gerade	*guhraaduh*	straight
gernhaben	*gernhahben*	to like
Geschäft, das	*guhschaeft, dass*	business; shop
geschlossen	*guhschlossen*	closed; shut
Geschwindigkeit, die	*guhschvindigkite, dee*	speed
Geschwür, das	*guhschvurrh, das*	ulcer
gestern	*gestern*	yesterday
gewinnen	*guhvinnen*	to win
gnädige Frau	*gnaydiguh frau*	madam
Golf	*gohlf*	golf
Golfplatz, der	*gohlfplatz, der*	golf course
gratis	*grahteece*	free (money)
Grippe, die	*grippuh, dee*	flu
groß	*grohss*	big; tall
Gruppe, die	*gruppuh, dee*	group
gültig	*gueltig*	valid
gut	*goot*	good; well

H

Haar, das	*haar, dass*	hair
haben	*hahben*	to have
Hafen, der	*haafen, der*	port (sea)
halb	*halp*	half
halten	*halten*	to keep
Handy, das	*hendy, dass*	mobile phone
hässlich	*hesslikh*	ugly
Haupt-	*howpt-*	main
heiß	*hice*	hot
helfen	*helfen*	to help
Herr	*herr*	sir
Herrentoilette, die	*herrentwighlettuh, dee*	gents
Herzlichen Glückwunsch!	*herzlikhen glueck-vunsch!*	congratulations!
heute	*hoytuh*	today
heute Abend/Nacht	*hoytuh ahbent/nakht*	tonight
hier	*heeuh*	here
Hilfe!	*hillfuh!*	help!
hinauf	*hinowf*	up
hinten	*hinten*	back (place)
hinunter	*hinunter*	down
Hitze, die	*hitzuh, dee*	heat
hoch, hohe/r/s	*hokh, hohhur/u/r/s*	high
homosexuell	*hohmozekszooell*	homosexual
hübsch	*huebsch*	pretty
hungrig sein	*hungrig zighn*	to be hungry

I

Identitätskarte, die	*eedentitaetskahrtuh, dee*	identity card
Ihr/e	*ihr/era*	your (formal)
Impfung, die	*impfung, dee*	vaccination
importieren	*importeerren*	to import

in	*in*	in
Information, die	*informatiohn, dee*	information
innen	*innen*	inside
Insel, die	*inzel, dee*	island
interessant	*interesssant*	interesting

international	*internatsional*	international

Berlin is a bubbling and cosmopolitan city, which attracts young, creative types from all over.

irgendein/e	*ihrgenteyn/uh*	any
irgendetwas	*ihrgentetvass*	something
Irisch	*ihrish*	Irish
Irland	*ihrlant*	Ireland

J

ja	*yaah*	yes
Jahr, das	*yahr, dass*	year
Jahrestag, der	*yahruhstaag, der*	anniversary
jährlich	*yerlikh*	yearly
Januar	*yanuar*	January
Jet-Ski, der	*jet-ski, der*	jet ski
jetzt	*yetzt*	now
Jugendherberge, die	*yugentherberguh, dee*	youth hostel

Juli	*yuhlee*	July

Switzerland hosts the world's biggest jazz stars each July at the **Montreux Jazz Festival**.

jung	*yung*	young
Junge, der	*yunguh, der*	boy
Juni	*yuhnee*	June

K

Kaffeehaus, das	*kaffayhowss, dass*	coffee house
kalt	*kalt*	cold
Kamera, die	*kamuhra, dee*	camera
Kartenschalter, der	*kartenschaltuh, der*	ticket office
Kartenverkauf, der	*kartenferkowf, der*	box office
Karton, der	*karton, der*	carton (cigarettes)
Kasse, die	*kassuh, dee*	cashpoint
Kassenzettel, der	*kassentsettel, der*	ticket (shopping)
Kathedrale, die	*kataydrahluh, dee*	cathedral
kaufen	*cowfen*	to buy
Kellner/in, der/die	*kellner/in, der/dee*	waiter/waitress
kennen	*kennen*	to know (person)
Kind, das	*kint, dass*	child; kid
Kinderbett, das	*kinderbett, dass*	cot
Kino, das	*keenoh, dass*	cinema
Kinofilm, der	*keenofeelm, der*	film (cinema)
Kiosk, der	*kiosk, der*	kiosk
Kleidung, die	*klydung, dee*	clothes
klein	*kline*	small
klopfen	*klopfen*	to knock
Kneipe, die	*kniypuh, dee*	pub

German	Pronunciation	English
Koffer, der	*koffuh, der*	suitcase
können	*kernen*	can (to be able)
Konsulat, das	*konzoolaat, dass*	consulate
kontaktieren	*kontakteerren*	to contact
kosten	*kosten*	to cost
Kosten, die	*kosten, dee*	cost
krank	*krank*	ill
Krankenhaus, das	*krankenhowss, dass*	hospital
Krankenwagen, der	*krankenvahgen, der*	ambulance
Kreditkarte, die	*kraydeetkartuh, dee*	credit card
kühl	*kewhl*	cool
Kunde, der	*kunduh, der*	customer

Kunst, die	*kunst, dee*	**art**

The **Kunsthaus Zürich** (Zurich Art Gallery) focuses on 19th- and 20th-century art. It houses Switzerland's most important art collection.

German	Pronunciation	English
kurz	*korz*	short
Kuss, der	*kuss, der*	kiss
küssen	*kuessen*	to kiss
Küste, die	*kueste, dee*	coast

L

Laden, der	*laaden, der*	shop
Land, das	*lant, dass*	country
Landschaft, die	*lantschaft, dee*	countryside
langsam	*langzaam*	slow
Lebensmittel-vergiftung, die	*lehbensmittel-fergiftung, dee*	food poisoning
legen	*lehgen*	to put; to lay
letzte/r/s	*letztuh/r/s*	last
Leute, die	*loytuh, dee*	people
Lieblings-	*leeblings-*	favourite
lokal	*lohkahl*	local
Luftpost, die	*luftposst, dee*	airmail

M

German	Pronunciation	English
machen	*makhen*	to make
Mädchen, das	*maidshen, das*	girl
Magengeschwür, das	*maagenguhschvurrh, das*	stomach ulcer
Mai	*my*	May
Manager, der	*manager, der*	manager
Mann, der	*man, der*	man
Marke, die	*markuh, dee*	stamp; label
Markt, der	*markt, der*	market
März	*mehrz*	March
Maut, die	*mowt, dee*	toll
Mechaniker, der	*mecaanikuh, der*	mechanic
Meer, das	*mehr, dass*	sea
Meeting, das	*meeting, das*	meeting
mehr	*mehr*	more
Mehrwertsteuer, die	*mehrvertstoyuh, dee*	VAT
mein/meine	*mine/mynuh*	my

meist/am meisten	*mighst/am mighsten*	most
Menge, die	*mengguh, dee*	quantity
Miete, die	*meetuh, dee*	rent
mieten	*meeten*	to hire; to rent
Mindest-	*mindest-*	minimum
Minute, die	*meenootuh, dee*	minute
mit (dem Flugzeug, dem Auto, etc.)	*mit (daym floogtsoyg, daym owtoe, etc.)*	with; by (air, car, etc)
Mittag, der	*mittaag, der*	midday
Mitternacht, die	*mitternahkt, dee*	midnight
Mobiltelefon, das	*mohbealtelefohn dass*	mobile phone
mögen	*mergen*	to like
möglich	*merglish*	possible
Moment, der	*mohment, der*	moment
morgen	*morgen*	tomorrow
Mücke, die	*mueckuh, dee*	mosquito
müde	*mewduh*	tired
Museum, das	*moozayum, dass*	museum
Musical, das	*moozikaal, das*	musical
müssen	*muessen*	must
Mutter, die	*muttuh, dee*	mother

N

nach	*nakh*	to
nach links/rechts/ oben	*nakh links/rekhts/ ohben*	to the left/right/ upstairs
Nachname, der	*nakhnahmuh, der*	surname
Nachricht, die	*nakhrischt, dee*	message
Nachrichten, die	*nakhrikhten, dee*	news
nächste/r/s	*nekhschtuh/ur/us*	next

Nacht, die	**nakht, dee**	**night**

Hamburg's famous nightlife district, **St Pauli**, is full of good bars, also frequented by locals.

Nachtklub, der	*nakhtklub, der*	nightclub
nahe/nahe bei	*nahhuh/nahhuh bye*	near/close by
Name, der	*nahmuh, der*	name
Nationalität, die	*natsionalitayte, dee*	nationality
neben	*nehben*	by (beside); next to
nehmen	*nehmen*	to take
nett	*nett*	nice; kind
neu	*noy*	new
nichts	*nikhts*	nothing
niemals	*neemals*	never
nirgendwo	*nihrgentvo*	nowhere
noch	*nokh*	still
noch eine/n/s	*nokh eyenuh/en/s*	another
Norden, der	*norden, der*	north
normalerweise	*normaaluhvysuh*	usually
Notaufnahme, die	*nohtowfnaahmuh, dee*	A&E
Notfall, der	*nohtfal, der*	emergency
notwendig	*nohtvendig*	necessary
November	*nofember*	November

Nudistenstrand	*noodistenschtrant*	nudist beach
null	*null*	zero
nur	*noor*	only; just
nützlich	*nuetzlikh*	useful

O

oben	*ohben*	up, upstairs
oder	*ohduh*	or
öffentliche Verkehr, der	*erfentlishuh ferkehr, der*	public transport
öffnen	*erfnen*	to open
ohne	*ohnnuh*	without
okay	*okay*	ok

Oktober	*oktohbuh*	October

There's only one place to be in October: **Auf der Wiesn** (on the meadow) at Germany's biggest beer festival, in Munich.

Optiker, der	*optikuh, der*	optician's
in Ordnung	*in ordnung*	all right
Ort, der	*ort, der*	place

P

Paar, das	*paar, dass*	pair
Park, der	*park, der*	park
parken	*parken*	to park
Parkplatz, der	*parkplatz, der*	parking
Party, die	*party, dee*	party
pensioniert	*punsiohneeeert*	retired
per	*per*	by (via)
Person, die	*perzohn, dee*	person
Personal, das	*perzonaal, das*	staff
Pfund Sterling	*pfunt schterling*	sterling pound
Platz, der	*platz, der*	place
plötzlich	*plertzlish*	suddenly
Polizei, die	*poleetsigh, dee*	police
Post, die	*posst, dee*	mail; post
Postamt, das	*posstamt, dass*	post office
Preis, der	*price, der*	price
privat	*preevaat*	private
Problem, das	*prohblehm, das*	problem

Q

Qualität, die	*qvalitayt, dee*	quality
Quiz, das	*qviz, dass*	quiz

R

Rabatt, der	*rabaat, der*	discount
Radio, das	*raadio, das*	radio
Radsport, der	*raadschport, der*	cycling
rasch	*rasch*	quick
Rasierklinge, die	*razeerklinguh, dee*	razor blade

Rathaus, das   *raat-howss, dass*   town hall
Vienna's City Hall hosts the yearly Life Ball, where celebrities from around the world gather for one of Europe's foremost AIDS fundraising events.

German	Pronunciation	English
rauben	*rowben*	to rob
rauchen	*rowhken*	to smoke
Rechenmaschine, die	*reschenmascheenuh, dee*	calculator
Rechnung, die	*rechnung, dee*	bill
Recht haben	*rekht hahben*	to be right
Regen, der	*rehgen, der*	rain
Regenschirm, der	*rehgenscheerm, der*	umbrella
Region, die	*raygeeohn, dee*	area
regional	*raygeeohnnal*	regional
Regionalkennzahl, die	*raygeeohnalkentsahl, dee*	area code
reich	*righkh*	rich
Reise, die	*righzuh, dee*	journey; travel
Reiseagentur, die	*righzuhahgentor, dee*	travel agency
Reiseführer, der	*righzuhfuehruh, der*	guide
Reisegepäck, das	*righzuhguhpeck, dass*	luggage
Reisepass, der	*righzuhpass, der*	passport
Reiseroute, die	*righzuhrootuh, dee*	itinerary
Reisverschluss, der	*riceferschluss, der*	zip
reiten	*righten*	to ride
rennen	*rennen*	to run
Reparaturwerkstatt, die	*repahraatorverkschtatt, dee*	garage (repairs)
reservieren	*reserveeren*	to reserve
Reservierung, die	*reserveerung, dee*	reservation
Rettungsschwimmer, der	*rettungsschvimmer, der*	lifeguard
Rettungsweste, die	*rettungsvestuh, dee*	life jacket
Rezept, das	*retsept, dass*	recipe
Rezeption, die	*retseptiohn, dee*	reception
Rezeptionist/in, der/die	*retseptiohnist/in, der/dee*	receptionist
richtig	*rikhtig*	true
Rollstuhl, der	*rohlschtool, der*	wheelchair
röntgen	*rerntgen*	to x-ray
Röntgenaufnahme, die	*rerntgenowfnahmuh, dee*	x-ray
Röntgenstrahlen, die	*rerntgenschtraahlen, dee*	x-rays
Route, die	*rootuh, dee*	route
Rückvergütung, die	*rueckferguetung, dee*	refund
rufen	*roofen*	to call
ruhig	*roohig*	quiet
Ruinen, die	*rooeenen, dee*	ruins
rund um	*runt um*	around

S

German	Pronunciation	English
Sahne, die	*zahnuh, dee*	cream
Sauerstoff, der	*zowuhschtoff, der*	oxygen
Sauna, die	*zowna, dee*	sauna
Schaden, der	*schaaden, der*	damage
schauen	*schowen*	to look
Scheck, der	*scheck, der*	cheque
schicken	*schicken*	to send
schlafen	*schlaafen*	to sleep
Schlaftablette, die	*schlaaftablettuh, dee*	sleeping pill
Schlange, die	*schlangguh, dee*	queue
schlecht	*schlekht*	bad; off (food)
schlechter	*schleshtuh*	worse
schließen	*schleessen*	to close

Schloss, das	*schloss, dass*	castle

Schloss Neuschwanstein, King Ludwig II of Bavaria's fairytale castle, is much more impressive in its original form than in Disneyworld!

German	Pronunciation	English
Schlüssel, der	*schluessel, der*	key
Schlüsselring, der	*schluesselring, der*	keyring
schmerzen	*schmerzen*	to hurt
Schmerzmittel, das	*schmerzmittel, dass*	painkiller
schmutzig	*schmutzig*	dirty
schneiden	*schnyden*	to cut
schnell	*schnell*	quick; quickly
Schnitt, der	*schnitt, der*	cut
schon	*schohn*	yet
Schottisch	*schotttish*	Scottish
Schottland	*schottlant*	Scotland
schreiben	*schrighben*	to write
Schwester, die	*schvesstuh, dee*	sister
schwierig	*schveerig*	difficult
Schwimmbad, das	*schvimmbaad, dass*	swimming pool
See, die	*zay, dee*	lake
sehr	*zehr*	very
sein	*zighn*	to be
seit	*zight*	since
Selbstbedienung, die	*zelbstbuhdeenung, dee*	self-service
senden	*zenden*	to send
September	*zeptembuh*	September
Service, der	*serveecesuh, der*	service
Show, die	*show, dee*	show
sich beschweren	*zikh buhschvehren*	to complain
sich übergeben	*zikh ewbuhgehben*	to vomit
sicher	*zishher*	safe
Sicherheitsgurt, der	*zisherheightsgort, der*	seat belt
Sie	*zee*	you (formal)
Sitz, der	*zitz, der*	seat
Ski, der	*schee, der*	ski
eine SMS senden	*eyenuh ess-m-ess zenden*	to text
sofort	*zofort*	immediately

Sohn, der	*zohn, der*	son
Sonne, die	*zonnuh, dee*	sun
Sonnenbrille, die	*zonnenbrilluh, dee*	sunglasses
Sorte, die	*zortuh, dee*	kind (sort)
spät	*spaet*	late (time)
Speisesaal, der	*schpighsuhzaal, der*	dining room

Sport, der	***schport, der***	**sport**

Combine sightseeing with sport: run the Berlin Marathon and
survey the city's most beautiful sights.

Sprache, die	*schpraachhuh, dee*	language
Sprachführer, der	*schprachfuehruh, der*	phrase book
Stadium, das	*schtaadium, dass*	stadium
Stadt, die	*schtadt, dee*	city; town
Stadtplan, der	*schtatplan, der*	map (city)
starten	*schtarten*	to start (car)
Station, die	*schtatiohn, dee*	station
stellen	*schtellen*	to put
Steuer, die	*schtoyuh, dee*	tax; duty
steuerfrei	*schtoyuhfry*	tax free
stören	*schtoeren*	to disturb
stornieren	*schtorneeren*	to cancel
Strafzettel, der	*straaftsettel, der*	ticket (parking)
Strand, der	*strant, der*	beach
Straße, die	*schtraassuh, dee*	road; street
Straßenbahn, die	*straassenbaahn, dee*	tram
Stress, der	*schtress, der*	stress
Südafrika	*zuedafreeka*	South Africa
Südafrikaner/in	*zuedafreekaanuh/in*	South African
Süden, der	*zueden, der*	south
sympathisch	*zympaatish*	nice (people)
Symptom, das	*zumptohm, dass*	symptom

T

Tabak, der	*tabak, der*	tobacco
Tag, der	*taag, der*	day
Tageszeitung, die	*taaguhstsighttung, dee*	newspaper
Tampons, die	*tampohns, dee*	tampons
Tankstelle, die	*tankschtelluh, dee*	filling (station)
Tastatur, die	*tasttator, dee*	keyboard
Taxi, das	*taxee, das*	taxi
Taxistand, der	*taxeeschtant, der*	taxi rank
Telefon, das	*telefohn, dass*	telephone
telefonieren	*telefohneeren*	to phone
Telefonist/in, der/die	*telefohnist/in, der/dee*	operator
Telefonzelle, die	*telefohnschtelluh, dee*	telephone box
Tennis	*tenneece*	tennis
Tennisplatz, der	*tenneeceplatz, der*	tennis court
Terrasse, die	*terrassuh, dee*	terrace
Tierpark, der	*teerpark, der*	zoo
Tisch, der	*tisch, der*	table
Tochter, die	*tokhtuh, dee*	daughter
Toilette, die	*twighlettuh, dee*	toilet

Toilettenartikel, die	*twighlettenarteekel, dee*	toiletries
töten	*terten*	to kill
treffen	*treffen*	to meet
Trinkgeld, das	*trinkgelt, dass*	tip (money)
trocken reinigen	*trocken rhinenigun*	to dry clean
typisch	*toopisch*	typical

U

U-Bahn, die	*oo-bahn, dee*	underground (tube)

Only four German cities (Berlin, Hamburg, Munich and Nuremberg) have an underground system.

über	*ewber*	about (concerning)
über Nacht	*ewber nahkt*	overnight
übernachten	*ewbernahkten*	to stay overnight
übersetzen	*ewberzetsen*	to translate
Uhrzeit, die	*uhrtsight, dee*	time (clock)
um	*um*	at (time)
Umkleidekabine, die	*umklyduhkahbeenuh, dee*	fitting room
unangenehm	*unanguhnehm*	unpleasant
unbequem	*unbuhgvehm*	uncomfortable
und	*unt*	and
Unfall, der	*unfal, der*	accident
unhöflich	*unhoeflikh*	rude
unten	*unten*	down
unter	*unter*	under
Unterkunft, die	*unterkunft, dee*	accommodation
unterschreiben	*unterschrighben*	to sign
Unterschrift, die	*unterschrift, dee*	signature
Unterwäsche, die	*untervaeschhuh, dee*	underwear

Urlaub, der	*uhrlowp, der*	holidays

Make sure your Viennese whirl includes a trip to a **Heurigen**. Often located in the city's vineyards, they serve young wine and typical Viennese food.

V

Vater, der	*fahtuh, der*	father
Vegetarier/in, der/die	*vegetaryer/in, der/dee*	vegetarian
Verabredung, die	*fehrappraydung, dee*	appointment
Verbrechen, das	*ferbreschen, dass*	crime
verfügbar	*ferfuegbar*	available
Vergewaltigung, die	*ferguhvaltigung, dee*	rape
verheiratet	*ferhighraatet*	married
verkaufen	*fercowfen*	to sell
verlieren	*ferleeren*	to lose
verlorene Gegenstände	*ferlorennuh gehgenschtenduh*	lost property

vermissen (eine Person)	_fermissen (eyenuh perzohn)_	to miss (a person)
vermisst	_fermisst_	missing
vernünftig	_fernuenftig_	sensible
verpassen (den Zug)	_ferpassen (deign tsoog)_	to miss (a train)
Versicherung, die	_fersisherung, dee_	insurance
verspätet	_ferspaetet_	late (delayed)
Verspätung, die	_ferspaetung, dee_	delay
verstehen	_ferstehen_	to understand
verweigern	_vervighgern_	to refuse
viel	_fiel_	much
viele	_feeluh_	many
vielleicht	_feellighscht_	maybe; perhaps
Viertel, das	_feartel, dass_	quarter
Visum, das	_veezum, dass_	visa
Vitamin, das	_vitameen, dass_	vitamin
von	_fon_	from
vor	_for_	ago

W

Wagen, der	_vahgen, der_	car
wählen	_vaylen_	to dial
wahr	_vahr_	true
während	_vehrrent_	during; while
wahrscheinlich	_vahrschineleesh_	probably
Währung, die	_vaehrung, dee_	currency
Wales	_vales_	Wales
Walisisch	_valeesish_	Welsh
wann?	_vann?_	when?
Wartezimmer, das	_wartuhtsimmuh, dass_	waiting room
warum?	_varrum?_	why?
was?	_vass?_	what?
waschen	_vaschen_	to wash
Waschsalon, der	_vashzallohn, der_	launderette
Wasser, das	_vasser, dass_	water
Wassersport, der	_vasserschport, der_	water sports
Web, das	_web, das_	web
Webseite, die	_webzightuh, dee_	website
Wechselbüro, das	_vechzellbyuroh, dass_	bureau de change
Wechselkurs, der	_vekhselcourse, der_	exchange rate
wechseln	_vechseln_	to change
Wecker, der	_vecker, der_	alarm
weg	_veck_	away
Weg, der	_veck, der_	way (route)
wegen	_vehgen_	because of
weich	_veikh_	soft
weit	_vight_	far
welche/r/s?	_velchuh/r/s?_	which?
Welt, die	_velt, dee_	world
weniger	_vehniguh_	less
wer?	_vehr?_	who?
Wert, der	_vert, der_	value
Wertsachen, die	_vertzakhen, dee_	valuables
weshalb?	_vesshalp?_	why?

German-English

Westen, der	*vesten, der*	west
Wetter, das	*vettuh, dass*	weather
wichtig	*vishtig*	important
wie?	*vee?*	how?
wie groß?	*vee grohss?*	how big?
wie lange?	*vee languh?*	how long?
wie weit?	*vee vight?*	how far?
wieder	*veeder*	again
wieviel?	*veefeel?*	how much?
willkommen	*villkommen*	welcome
wirklich	*virklish*	real
wissen	*vissen*	to know (knowledge)
wo?	*vo?*	where?
Woche, die	*vochhuh, dee*	week
Wochenende, das	*vochhenendduh, dass*	weekend
Wochentag, der	*vochentaag, der*	weekday
wollen	*vollen*	to want
Wort, das	*vort, dass*	word
wunderbar	*vunderbah*	wonderful
Wünsch, die	*voonsh, dee*	wish
wünschen	*voonshen*	to wish

Y

| Yacht, die | *yacht, dee* | yacht |

Z

Zahl, die	*tsaahl, dee*	number
zahlen	*tsaahlen*	to pay
Zahn, der	*tsahn, der*	tooth
zählen	*tsehlen*	to count
zanken	*tsanken*	to squabble
Zebrastreifen, der	*der tsaybraschtryfen*	zebra crossing
Zeichen, das	*tsighchen, dass*	sign
zeigen	*tsighgen*	to show
Zeit, die	*tsight, dee*	time
Zelt, das	*tselt, das*	tent
Zentrum, das	*tsentroom, dass*	centre
zickig	*tsikig*	touchy
ziemlich	*tseemlikh*	quite
Zigarette, die	*tsigarrettuh, dee*	cigarette
Zigarre, die	*tsigarruh, dee*	cigar
Zimmer, das	*tsimmuh, dass*	room
zirka	*tseerka*	circa; around
Zoll, der	*tsohl, der*	customs
Zone, die	*tsohnuh, dee*	zone
Zoo, der	*tsoh, der*	zoo
zu	*tsu*	to
Zug, der	*tsoog, der*	train
zuhören	*tsuhoerren*	to listen to
Zukunft, die	*tsukunft, dee*	future
zürück	*tsurook*	back (return)
zusammen	*tsuzammen*	together
zwingen	*tsvingen*	to force
zwingend	*tsvingend*	urgent
zwischen	*tsvischen*	between

Quick reference

Numbers

0	**null**	*nuull*
1	**eins**	*eyns*
2	**zwei**	*tsvigh*
3	**drei**	*dry*
4	**vier**	*fear*
5	**fünf**	*fuenf*
6	**sechs**	*zekhs*
7	**sieben**	*zeeben*
8	**acht**	*akht*
9	**neun**	*noyn*
10	**zehn**	*tsane*
11	**elf**	*elf*
12	**zwölf**	*tsvulf*
13	**dreizehn**	*drytsane*
14	**vierzehn**	*feartsane*
15	**fünfzehn**	*fuenftsane*
16	**sechzehn**	*zekhtsane*
17	**siebzehn**	*zeebtsane*
18	**achtzehn**	*achstsane*
19	**neunzehn**	*noyntsane*
20	**zwanzig**	*tsvantsig*
21	**einundzwanzig**	*eyn-unt-tsvantsig*
30	**dreißig**	*dryssig*
40	**vierzig**	*feartsig*
50	**fünfzig**	*fuenftsig*
60	**sechzig**	*zekhtsig*
70	**siebzig**	*zeebtsig*
80	**achtzig**	*akhtsig*
90	**neunzig**	*noyntsig*
100	**hundert**	*hundert*
1000	**tausend**	*towzent*
1st	**der/die/das erste**	*der/dee/dass erstuh*
2nd	**der/die/das zweite**	*der/dee/dass tsvightuh*
3rd	**der/die/das dritte**	*der/dee/dass drittuh*
4th	**der/die/das vierte**	*der/dee/dass feartuh*
5th	**der/die/das fünfte**	*der/dee/das fuenftuh*

Weights & measures

gram (=0.03oz)	**das Gramm**	*dass gram*
kilogram (=2.2lb)	**das Kilogramm**	*dass keelogram*
pound (=0.45kg)	**das Pfund**	*dass pfunt*
centimetre (=0.4in)	**der Zentimeter**	*der tsenteemaytuh*
metre (=1.1yd)	**der Meter**	*der maytuh*
kilometre (=0.6m)	**der Kilometer**	*der keelomaytuh*
litre (=2.1pt)	**der Liter**	*der leetuh*

Days & time

Monday	**Montag**	*mohntaag*
Tuesday	**Dienstag**	*deenschtaag*
Wednesday	**Mittwoch**	*mittvokh*
Thursday	**Donnerstag**	*dohnuhschtaag*
Friday	**Freitag**	*frytaag*
Saturday	**Samstag**	*zamschtaag*
Sunday	**Sonntag**	*zonntaag*

What time is it?	**Wie spät ist es?**	*vee schpayt isst es?*
(Four) o'clock	**(Vier) Uhr**	*(fear) ohr*
Quarter past (six)	**Viertel nach (sechs)**	*fiertel nakh (zekhs)*
Half past (eight)	**Halb (neun)**	*halp (noyn)*
Quarter to (ten)	**Viertel vor (zehn)**	*fiertel for (tsane)*
morning	**Morgen**	*moorgen*
afternoon	**Nachmittag**	*nakhmittaag*
evening	**Abend**	*ahbent*
night	**Nacht**	*nakht*

Clothes size conversions

Women's clothes	34	36	38	40	42	44	46	5C
equiv. UK size	6	8	10	12	14	16	18	2C

Men's jackets	44	46	48	50	52	54	56	58
equiv. UK size	34	36	38	40	42	44	46	48

Men's shirts	36	37	38	39	40	41	42	43
equiv. UK size	14	14.5	15	15.5	16	16.5	17	17.

Shoes	36.5	37.5	39	40	41.5	42.5	44	45
equiv. UK size	4	5	6	7	8	9	10	11